Java™

PHRASEBOOK

ESSENTIAL CODE AND COMMANDS

Timothy Fisher

Sams Publishing, 800 East 96th Street, Indianapolis, Indiana 46240 USA

Java™ Phrasebook

International Standard Book Number: 0-672-32907-7

Library of Congress Catalog Card Number: 2006921449

Printed in the United States of America

First Printing: November 2006

09 08 07 06 4 3 2 1

Trademarks

Warning and Disclaimer

Bulk Sales

Acquisitions Editors
Jenny Watson
Mark Taber

Development Editor
Songlin Qiu

Managing Editor
Patrick Kanouse

Project Editor
Mandie Frank

Copy Editor
Rhonda Tinch-Mize

Indexer
Tim Wright

Proofreader
Susan Eldridge

Technical Editor
Boris Minkin

Publishing Coordinator
Vanessa Evans

Book Designer
Gary Adair

Table of Contents

About the Author

Timothy Fisher has been working professionally in the Java software development field since 1997. He has served in a variety of roles including developer, team leader, and chief architect. Tim is currently a consultant for the Compuware Corporation in Detroit, Michigan. Tim also enjoys writing about technology and has been a contributor to *Java Developer's Journal* and *XML Journal*. Along with his technology interests, Tim is also passionate about education and the use of advanced Internet technologies for education. You can contact Tim and read his blog at: www.timothyfisher.com.

Dedication

This book is dedicated to my parents Thomas and Betty Fisher. They have been my foundation throughout my life. Without them I would not be where I am today.

Acknowledgments

I would like to acknowledge everyone who helped me in getting this book done. First of all I would like to thank the staff at Pearson for sticking with me and guiding me through this project. I have written many articles and papers, but I am a first-time author when it comes to book writing. Despite many missed deadlines and delays in writing, the editors stuck with me and helped me to assure that my first book project was indeed successful. The editors that I interacted with, Songlin Qiu and Mandie Frank, were very helpful throughout the process. I'd also like to thank the technical editor, Boris Minkin, who was also a big part of this project. He provided needed technical review to make sure what I was saying was correct. In a book like this, there are many opportunities for errors and without the work of Boris Minkin, the book quality would have suffered.

Finally, I'd like to thank my family, Kerry, Timmy, and Camden who provided me encouragement and complete support in writing this book and thus accomplishing a significant goal of mine. My wife, Kerry, stepped in to take over most of the household chores while I dedicated many evenings to completing this book. Timmy and Camden settled for a little less play time with Dad. Finally, without my parents, Tom and Betty Fisher, I wouldn't be where I am today. They have been my foundation and inspiration in life. Kerry, Timmy, Camden, and Mom and Dad, I love you all…

We Want to Hear from You!

As the reader of this book, *you* are our most important critic and commentator. We value your opinion and want to know what we're doing right, what we could do better, what areas you'd like to see us publish in, and any other words of wisdom you're willing to pass our way.

You can email or write me directly to let me know what you did or didn't like about this book—as well as what we can do to make our books stronger.

Please note that I cannot help you with technical problems related to the topic of this book, and that due to the high volume of mail I receive, I might not be able to reply to every message.

When you write, please be sure to include this book's title and author as well as your name and phone or email address. I will carefully review your comments and share them with the author and editors who worked on the book.

Email: webdev@samspublishing.com

Mail: Mark Taber
Associate Publisher
Sams Publishing
800 East 96th Street
Indianapolis, IN 46240 USA

Reader Services

Visit our website and register this book at www.samspublishing.com/register for convenient access to any updates, downloads, or errata that might be available for this book.

Introduction

Earlier this year, I was asked by an editor at Pearson to write this phrasebook focused on Java. It is one of several in their Phrasebook series. Christian Wenz wrote the first one in the series, the *PHP Phrasebook*. The concept for the phrasebook series comes from the foreign language phrasebooks. Foreign language phrasebooks contain a list of common phrases that you might want to say in the foreign language. These books are very useful for visitors who do not know the local language. The concept of technical phrasebooks is similar. They show the reader how to accomplish common tasks using the technology which is the subject of the book.

The goal of this phrasebook is to provide you with a guide book of commonly used Java programming phrases. This book should be useful to both the seasoned Java programmer and the programmer who is new to Java. Although the book can be read cover-to-cover to get a good overview of the Java language, the book is best used as an on-hand reference when the programmer wants to know how to accomplish a common task in the Java language. You may also wish to explore the book to discover some Java features and techniques that you may not have been aware of before.

The book is not a Java language tutorial or introduction, nor is it a complete reference to the Java language. There are many more classes and APIs than what you will find covered in this book. There are already many excellent learning Java style books and Java reference books covering pretty much every technology you can think of. If your goal is to get a deeper understanding of a specific technology, this is not the book you are looking for.

Most of the phrases and sample code shown in this book do not contain error handling code. Many of the phrases may throw exceptions that you will have to handle in any real applications that you write. The error and exception handling code is not shown in this book so that the reader can focus on the purpose of the phrase or sample code without being distracted by a lot of error handling code. When you include all of the standard exception handling in a code sample, the phrase can quickly become something much more than a short concise phrase, and yet showing all of the exception handling code will not have helped you to understand the specific phrase any better. Not showing the error handling code allows the phrases to be kept short and concise. The JavaDoc for the Java JDK is an excellent source for looking up which exceptions can be thrown by any method contained in the Java classes that you will come across in this book. You can access the JavaDoc at: http://java.sun.com/j2se/1.5.0/docs/api/.

The phrases contained in this book should be OS independent. The Java platform's motto of write-once-run-anywhere should apply to all of the phrases and sample code contained in this book. The phrases were tested under JDK 1.5, also referred to as Java 5.0. Most of the phrases will work well under earlier versions of the JDK as well, except where noted.

All of the phrases and sample code in this book have been tested and should be error-free. While my hope is that this book is 100% error-free, I do realize that most technical books don't quite meet that mark. Any errors and other errata that are found will be made available on www.samspublishing.com.

While writing this book, I have tried to come up with what I considered to be the most useful phrases while maintaining the concise format of the Phrasebook series. I am certain that at some point you will be looking for a certain phrase that you will not find in this book. If you feel that a phrase should be included in this book, I'd like to hear from you. Also, if you feel that there are phrases contained in this book which are less than useful, please tell me that as well. As a writer, I always enjoy feedback from my readers. Perhaps at some point in the future you will see a second edition of this book that takes your feedback into account. You can reach me through my website at www.timothyfisher.com.

There is more to Java, of course, than can be covered in a book this size. When you register this book at www.samspublishing.com/register, you will find additional material as well as any updates.

1

The Basics

This chapter contains the phrases that you will need to get you started in Java development. These are things that you need to know before you can accomplish much of anything in Java. The basics include compiling and running your Java code, and understanding the Java class path. Unlike languages such as PHP and Basic, Java source code must be compiled into what is called byte code before it can be executed. The compiler places the byte code into Java class files. Therefore, it is important for anyone programming in Java to understand how to compile their source code into class files, and then be able to execute those class files. Knowledge of the Java class path is important for both compiling and executing Java code. Therefore it is with these phrases that we start.

Today it is common to do Java development within an integrated development environment (IDE), such as the freely available Eclipse project—see http://www.eclipse.org. This chapter assumes that you are performing the tasks at the command line. Although realistically, you might use an IDE for most of your development, every developer should be familiar with setting up and accomplishing these tasks outside the IDE. Performing these tasks within the IDE will vary with the IDE, and references for your particular IDE are the best place to go for that help.

To execute the phrases contained in this chapter, you should obtain a Java distribution from Sun. Sun makes Java technology available in several popular forms. The most common Java distributions are the Java Standard Edition (SE), the Java Enterprise Edition (EE), and the Java Micro Edition (ME). To complete all phrases in this book, you will only need the Java SE package. Java EE contains additional features for developing enterprise applications, and the Java ME is geared towards developing applications for devices such as cell phones and PDAs. All of these packages can be downloaded from the Sun Java website at http://java.sun.com. The J2SE 5.0 is the most recent version of the Java SE at the time of this writing. Unless you have a reason to use a previous version, this is the version you should use with this book. Within the J2SE 5.0, you will find two packages available for download, the JDK and the JRE. The JDK is the Java development kit and is what you will need to develop Java applications. The JRE is the Java runtime edition and will only allow you to run Java applications, but not build your own. So for this book you will need the JDK distribution of the J2SE 5.0 package.

NOTE: J2SE 5.0 and JDK 5.0 are also often referred to as JDK 1.5. Sun decided to officially change the name of the 1.5 version to 5.0.

For assistance in installing the most recent version of the Java J2SE JDK as of the writing of this book, see http://java.sun.com/j2se/1.5.0/install.html.

Compiling a Java Program

```
javac HelloWorld.java
```

In this phrase, we compile the `HelloWorld.java` source file to bytecode. Bytecode is Java's platform-independent representation of a program's instructions. The output will be placed in the `HelloWorld.class` file.

The `javac` executable is included with the Java JDK distribution. This javac program is used to compile the Java source files that you write into Java class files. A java class file is a bytecode representation of the compiled java source. For more complete information about the `javac` command, be sure to see the JDK documentation. There are many options you can use with `javac` that are not covered in this book.

For most programming projects, other than very small and simple programs, you will most likely use an IDE or a tool, such as the Ant build tool from Apache, to perform your compiling. If you are compiling anything other than a very small project with minimal source files, I highly recommend that you become familiar with Ant. If you are familiar with the Make build tool commonly used by C programmers, you will understand the importance of Ant. Ant is like a Make tool for Java. With Ant you can create a build script that will allow you to specify details of how a complex application should be built, and with a single command you can automatically build the entire application. You can get more information about Ant and download it from http://ant.apache.org.

Running a Java Program

```
javac HelloWorld.java  // compile source file
java HelloWorld  // execute byte code
```

In this phrase, we first use the javac compiler to compile our Java source into a HelloWorld.class file. Then, we can execute the HelloWorld program using the java command and passing the name of the compiled class, HelloWorld. Note that you do not include the .class extension when passing the name to the java command.

The java executable is included with either the Java JDK distribution or the Java JRE distribution. This program is used to execute your compiled Java class files. The Java executable can be thought of as the interpreter that compiles your bytecode real-time into executable native code that runs on the platform you are executing on. The Java executable is a platform dependent piece of Java. Each platform that supports Java will have its own Java executable compiled specifically for that platform. This piece of Java is also called the virtual machine.

Setting the Classpath

```
set CLASSPATH = /user/projects/classes
java -classpath =
    CLASSPATH%;classes/classa.class;libs/stuff.jar
```

The classpath is used by the java executable and the java compiler to find the compiled class files and any libraries packaged as JAR files required to run or compile a program. JAR files are the standard way of packaging libraries into a single file resource. The preceding phrase shows how the classpath can be set when executing a java program at the command line. By default, the classpath is obtained from the operating system `CLASSPATH` environment variable. In the phrase, a specific class, `classfile.class`, located in the `classes` directory, is appended to the classpath set by the environment variable. A library called `stuff.jar`, located in the `libs` directory, is also appended to the classpath.

If the `CLASSPATH` environment variable is not set, and the `-classpath` option is not used, the classpath defaults to the current directory. If you do set the classpath using either of these options, the current directory is not automatically included in the classpath. This is a common source of problems. If you are setting the classpath, you must explicitly add the current directory. You can add the current directory to the classpath by specifying it as "." in the classpath.

CAUTION: Note that while any classes are found in a directory that is included in the classpath, JAR files must be explicitly included in the classpath to be found. They will not be found just by including the directory in which they reside, in the classpath.

Classpath-related problems are very common among novice and even experienced programmers, and can often be very frustrating to solve. If you take the time to fully understand the classpath and how to set it, then you should be able to avoid these types of problems in your applications. For additional information about setting and using the classpath, see this URL - http://java.sun.com/j2se/1.5.0/docs/tooldocs/windows/classpath.html.

2

Interacting with the Environment

This chapter provides phrases that help you interact with the runtime environment which your Java application is executing in. Many of the phrases in this chapter make use of the Java `System` object. The `System` object is a core Java object intended for interacting with the environment surrounding your Java application. You should take special caution when using this object and in general when interacting with the environment, for if you are not careful, this can lead to platform dependent code. This is because the System object interacts with the environment, which may be different depending on the platform you are working on. So the results of using a System method or property on one platform may not be consistent across all platforms.

Getting Environment Variables

```
String envPath = System.getenv("PATH");
```

This phrase shows how you can retrieve an environment variable using the `System.getenv()` method. This method was deprecated in versions of JDK 1.2 through 1.4. In JDK 1.5, Sun did something that they don't do too often and they undeprecated this method. If you are using a version of the JDK that has this method deprecated, at compile time, you will get deprecation warnings if you attempt to use this method. A deprecated method is a method that should not be used in new development projects, but is supported for backward compatibility purposes. There is no guarantee that deprecated methods will continue to be supported in future versions of the JDK. But again, in the case of this method, in the most recent version of the JDK, 1.5, the method is not deprecated, so you can probably assume that it will indeed continue to be supported.

In general, it is usually considered a bad practice to rely on environment variables in your Java application. This is because environment variables are a platform-dependent concept, and Java strives to be platform independent. Some Java platforms, most notably the Macintosh, do not even have the concept of environment variables; thus in these environments, your code would not behave as expected. The next phrase describes how to get and set system properties. This approach is preferred over using environment variables.

Setting and Getting System Properties

```
System.setProperty("timezone",
"EasternStandardTime");
String zone = System.getProperty("timezone");
```

System properties are key/value pairs that are external to your Java application. The Java `System` object provides a mechanism for reading the names and values of these external system properties into your Java application. The preceding phrase shows how you can set and get a system property using the Java `System` object.

You can also retrieve all the system properties into a properties object using the following statement:

```
Properties systemProps = System.getProperties();
```

There is also a method for retrieving just the system property names. The following code snippet shows how you can retrieve all the system property names and then retrieve each property using its name:

```
Properties props = System.getProperties();
Enumeration propertyNames = props.propertyNames();
String key = "";
while (propertyNames.hasMoreElements()) {
     key = (String) propertyNames.nextElement();
     System.out.println(key + "=" +
         props.getProperty(key));
}
```

Parsing Command-Line Arguments

```
java my_program arg1 arg2 arg3

public static void main(String[] args) {
    String arg1 = args[0];
    String arg2 = args[1];
    String arg3 = args[2];
}
```

In this phrase, we store the values of three command line arguments into three separate string variables, `arg1`, `arg2`, and `arg3`.

Any java class can have a `main()` method, which is executable from the command line. The `main()` method accepts a `String` array of command-line arguments. The arguments are contained in the array in the order in which they are entered at the command line. So, to retrieve the command-line arguments, you simply have to extract the elements of the arguments array passed into the `main()` method.

If your application uses a lot of command-line arguments, it is wise to spend the time to write a custom command-line arguments parser to understand and handle various types of command-line arguments, such as single-character parameters, parameters that being with a dash (-), parameters that are immediately followed by another related parameter, and so on.

NOTE: Online, you can find many good examples of command-line argument processors to save you a lot of work. Here are two good libraries that can get you started:

http://jargs.sourceforge.net

https://args4j.dev.java.net/

Both of these are small libraries that can parse complex command-line arguments through a relatively simple interface.

3

Manipulating Strings

Much of what you do in any programming language involves the manipulation of strings. Other than numeric data, nearly all data is accessed as a string. Quite often, even numeric data is treated as a simple string. It is difficult to imagine being able to write a complete program without making use of strings.

The phrases in this chapter show you some common tasks involving strings. The Java language has strong built-in support for strings and string processing. Unlike the C language, strings are built-in types in the Java language. Java contains a `String` class that is used to hold string data. Strings in Java should not be thought of as an array of characters as they are in C. Whenever you want to represent a string in Java, you should use the `String` class, not an array.

An important property of the `String` class in Java is that once created, the string is immutable. This means that once created, a Java `String` object cannot be changed. You can reassign the name you've given a string to another string object, but you cannot change the string's contents. Because of this, you will not find any set methods in the String class. If you want to create a string that you can add data to, such as you might in some routine that builds up a string, you should use the StringBuilder class if you are using JDK 1.5, or the StringBuffer class in older versions of Java, instead of the String class. The StringBuilder and StringBuffer classes are mutable; thus you are allowed to change their contents. It is very common to build strings using the StringBuilder or StringBuffer class and to pass or store strings using the String class.

Comparing Strings

```
boolean result = str1.equals(str2);
boolean result2 = str1.equalsIgnoreCase(str2);
```

The value of result and result2 will be true if the strings contain the same content. If the strings contain different content, the value of result and result2 will be false. The first method, equals(), is case sensitive. The second method, equalsIgnoreCase(),will ignore the case of the strings and return true if the content is the same regardless of case.

String comparison is a common source of bugs for novice Java programmers. A novice programmer will often attempt to compare strings using the comparison operator ==. When used with Strings, the comparison operator == compares object references, not the contents of the object. Because of this, two string objects that contain the same string data, but are physically distinct string object instances, will not compare as equal when using the comparison operator.

The `equals()` method on the `String` class compares a string's contents, rather than its object reference. This is the preferred string comparison behavior in most string comparison cases. See the following example:

```
String name1 = new String("Timmy");
String name2 = new String("Timmy");
if (name1 == name2) {
     System.out.println("The strings are equal.");
}
else {
     System.out.println("The strings are not
equal.");
}
```

The output from executing these statements will be

```
The strings are not equal.
```

Now use the `equals()` method and see the results:

```
String name1 = new String("Timmy");
String name2 = new String("Timmy");
if (name1.equals(name2)) {
     System.out.println("The strings are equal.");
}
else {
     System.out.println("The strings are not
equal.");
}
```

The output from executing these statements will be

```
The strings are equal.
```

Another related method on the `String` class is the `compareTo()` method. The `compareTo()` method compares two strings lexographically, returning an integer value—either positive, negative, or `0`. The value `0` is returned only if the `equals()` method would evaluate to `true` for the two strings. A negative value is returned if the string on which the method is called alphabetically precedes the string that is passed as a parameter to the method. A positive value is returned if the string on which the method is called alphabetically comes after the string that is passed as a parameter. To be precise, the comparison is based on the Unicode value of each character in the strings being compared. The `compareTo()` method also has a corresponding `compareToIgnoreCase()` method that performs functionally the same with the exception that the characters' case is ignored. See the following example:

```
String name1="Camden";
String name2="Kerry";
int result = name1.compareTo(name2);
if (result == 0) {
     System.out.println("The names are equal.");
}
else if (result > 0) {
     System.out.println(
         "name2 comes before name1 alphabeti-
cally.");
}
else if (result < 0) {
     System.out.println(
        "name1 comes before name2 alphabetically.");
}
```

The output of this code will be

```
name1 comes before name2 alphabetically.
```

Searching For and Retrieving Substrings

```
int result = string1.indexOf(string2);
int result = string1.indexOf(string2, 5);
```

In the first method shown, the value of `result` will contain the index of the first occurrence of `string2` within `string1`. If `string2` is not contained within `string1`, `-1` will be returned.

In the second method shown, the value of `result` will contain the index of the first occurrence of `string2` within `string1` that occurs after the fifth character within `string1`. The second parameter can be any valid integer greater than `0`. If the value is greater than the length of `string1`, a result of `-1` will be returned.

Besides searching a string for a substring, there might be times when you know where a substring is that you are interested in and simply want to get at that substring. So, in either case, you now know where a substring is that you are interested in. Using the String's `substring()` method, you can now get that substring. The `substring()` method is overloaded, meaning that there are multiple ways of calling it. One way of calling it is to pass a start index. This will return a substring that begins at the start index and extends through the end of the string. The other way of using `substring()` is to call it with two parameters—a start index, and an end index.

```
String string1 = "My address is 555 Big Tree Lane";
String address = string1.substring(14);
System.out.println(address);
```

This code will print out

```
555 Big Tree Lane
```

The first `5` character is at position 14 in the string; thus it is the beginning of the substring. Note that strings are always zero-based indexed, and the last character of a string is at location (length of string) `-1`.

Processing a String One Character at a Time

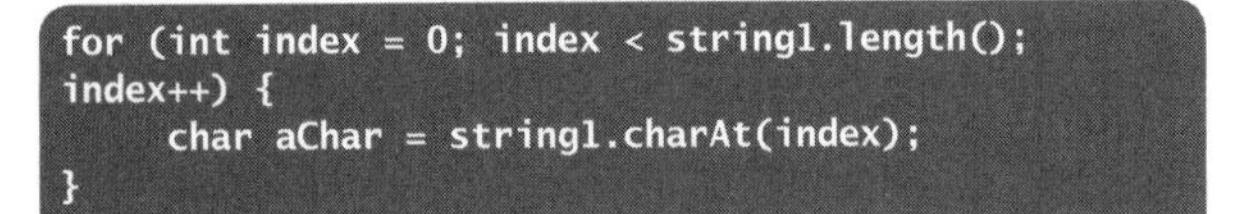

```
for (int index = 0; index < string1.length();
index++) {
     char aChar = string1.charAt(index);
}
```

The `charAt()` method allows you to obtain a single character from the string at the specified index. The characters are indexed 0 based, from 0 to the length of the string-1. The phrase shown previously loops through each character contained in `string1`.

An alternative method would be to use the `StringReader` class, as follows:

```
StringReader reader = new StringReader(string1);
int singleChar = reader.read();
```

Using this mechanism, the `read()` method of the `StringReader` class returns one character at a time, as an integer. Each time the `read()` method is called, the next character of the string will be returned.

Reversing a String by Character

```
String letters = "ABCDEF";
StringBuffer lettersBuff = new StringBuffer(let-
ters);
String lettersRev =
lettersBuff.reverse().toString();
```

The `StringBuffer` class contains a `reverse()` method that returns a `StringBuffer` that contains the characters from the original `StringBuffer` reversed. A `StringBuffer` is easily converted into a `String` using the `toString()` method of the `StringBuffer`. So by temporarily making use of a `StringBuffer`, you are able to produce a second string with the characters of an original string in reverse order.

If you are using JDK 1.5, you can use the `StringBuilder` class instead of the `StringBuffer` class. The `StringBuilder` class has an API compatible with the `StringBuffer` class. The `StringBuilder` class will give you faster performance, but its methods are not synchronized; thus it is not thread-safe. In multithreaded situations, you should continue to use the `StringBuffer` class.

Reversing a String by Word

```
String test = "Reverse this string";
Stack  stack = new Stack();
StringTokenizer strTok = new StringTokenizer(test);

while(strTok.hasMoreTokens()) {
    stack.push(strTok.nextElement());
}
```

```
StringBuffer revStr = new StringBuffer();
while(!stack.empty()) {
    revStr.append(stack.pop());
    revStr.append(" ");
}
System.out.println("Original string: " + test);
System.out.println("\nReversed string: " + revStr);
```

The output of this code fragment will be

```
Original string: Reverse this string
Reversed string: string this Reverse
```

As you can see, reversing a string by word is more complex than reversing a string by character. This is because there is built-in support for reversing a string by character, but there is no such built-in support for reversing by word. To accomplish this task, we make use of the `StringTokenizer` and the `Stack` classes. Using `StringTokenizer`, we parse each word out of the string and push it onto our stack. After we've processed the entire string, we iterate through the stack, popping each word off and appending to a string buffer that holds the reversed string. A stack that has the property of last item in becomes the first item out. Because of this property, the stack is often referred to as a LIFO (last in, first out) queue. This makes the reverse successful.

See the phrase covered in the section, "Parsing a Comma-Separated String" in this chapter for more uses of the `StringTokenizer` class.

NOTE: I don't cover it here, but you may also be interested in checking out a new addition to JDK 1.5, the Scanner class. The Scanner class is a simple text scanner which can parse primitive types and strings using regular expressions.

Making a String All Uppercase or All Lowercase

```
String string = "Contains some Upper and some
Lower.";
String string2 = string.toUpperCase();
String string3 = string.toLowerCase();
```

These two methods transform a string into all uppercase or all lowercase letters. They both return the transformed result. These methods do not change the original string. The original string remains intact with mixed case.

A practical area in which these methods are useful is when storing information in a database. There might be certain fields that you always want to store as all uppercase or all lowercase. These methods make the conversion a snap.

Case conversion is also useful for processing user logins. The user ID field is normally considered to be a field that's not case sensitive, whereas the password field is case sensitive. So, when comparing the user ID, you should convert to a known case and then compare to a stored value. Alternatively, you can always use the `equalsIgnoreCase()` method of the `String` class, which performs a non case sensitive comparison.

Trimming Spaces from the Beginning or End of a String

```
String result = str.trim();
```

The `trim()` method will remove both leading and trailing whitespace from a string and return the result.

The original string will remain unchanged. If there is no leading or trailing whitespace to be removed, the original string is returned. Both spaces and tab characters will be removed.

This is very useful when comparing user input with existing data. A programmer often racks his brain for hours trying to figure out why what he enters is not the same as a stored string, only to find out that the difference is only a trailing space. Trimming data prior to comparison will eliminate this problem.

Parsing a Comma-Separated String

```
String str = "tim,kerry,timmy,camden";
String[] results = str.split(",");
```

The `split()` method on the `String` class accepts a regular expression as its only parameter, and will return an array of `String` objects split according to the rules of the passed-in regular expression. This makes parsing a comma-separated string an easy task. In this phrase, we simply pass a comma into the `split()` method, and we get back an array of strings containing the comma-separated data. So the results array in our phrase would contain the following content:

```
results[0] = tim
results[1] = kerry
results[2] = timmy
results[3] = camden
```

Another useful class for taking apart strings is the `StringTokenizer` class. We will repeat the phrase using the StringTokenizer class instead of the split() method.

```
String str = "tim,kerry,timmy,Camden";
StringTokenizer st = new StringTokenizer(str, ",");
while (st.hasMoreTokens()) {
     System.out.println(st.nextToken());
}
```

This code example will print each of the names contained in the original string, str, on a separate line, as follows:

```
tim
kerry
timmy
camden
```

Notice that the commas are discarded and not output.

The StringTokenizer class can be constructed with one, two, or three parameters. If called with just one parameter, the parameter is the string that you want to tokenize, or split up. In this case, the delimiter is defaulted to natural word boundaries. The tokenizer uses the default delimiter set, which is " \t\n\r\f": the space character, the tab character, the newline character, the carriage-return character, and the form-feed character.

The second way of constructing a StringTokenizer object is to pass two parameters to the constructor. The first parameter is the string to be tokenized, and the second parameter is a string containing the delimiters that you want to split the string on. This overrides the default delimiters and sets them to whatever you pass in the second argument.

Finally, you can pass a third argument to the StringTokenizer constructor that designates whether delimiters should be returned as tokens or discarded. This is a Boolean parameter. A value of true passed here will cause the delimiters to be returned as tokens. False is the default value, which discards the delimiters and does not treat them as tokens.

You should also review the phrases in Chapter 6. With the addition of regular expression support to Java in JDK1.4, many of the uses of the `StringTokenizer` class can be replaced with regular expressions. The official JavaDoc states that the `StringTokenizer` class is a legacy class and its use should be discouraged in new code. Wherever possible, you should use the `split()` method of the `String` class or the regular expression package.

4

Working with Data Structures

A data structure is a mechanism for organizing data used by your program. Whenever you are working with groups of similar data items, it's a good idea to make use of a data structure. Java contains excellent built-in support for many different types of data structures, including arrays, lists, maps, and sets. Java bundles most of its classes for working with data structures into what is called the Collections Framework. The Collections Framework is a unified architecture for representing and manipulating collections or data structures. The most commonly used data structure classes are the `ArrayList` and the `HashMap`, and those classes are being focused on most in the phrases in this chapter.

The term data structures can apply to the way data is structured in a file or database as well as in-memory. All the phrases in this chapter deal with in-memory data structures.

NOTE: Sun makes available a document that gives a good overview of the Collections Framework along with some tutorials on how to use the various classes. You can view this document at this link: http://java.sun.com/j2se/1.5.0/docs/guide/collections/index.html

Resizing an Array

```
// use an ArrayList
List myArray = new ArrayList();
```

In Java, regular arrays of objects or primitives can not be dynamically resized. If you want an array larger than what was originally declared, you'd have to declare a new larger array and copy the contents from the original array to the new larger array. Here we show how this is accomplished:

```
int[] tmp = new int[myArray.length + 10];
System.arraycopy(myArray, 0, tmp, 0,
myArray.length);
myArray = tmp;
```

In this example, we have an array of integers called `myArray`, and we want to expand the size of the array by 10 elements. We create a new array, which we call `tmp`, and initialize it to the length of myArray + 10. We then use the `System.arrayCopy()` method to copy the contents of `myArray` to the `tmp` array. Finally, we set `myArray` to point to the newly created `tmp` array.

Generally, the best solution to this problem is to use an `ArrayList` object instead of a traditional array of objects. An `ArrayList` can hold any type of objects, and the major advantage of using it is that it dynamically resizes itself when necessary. With an `ArrayList`, you don't have to worry about the size of your array and whether you will run out of space. The ArrayList implementation is also much more efficient than using the method described previously to copy an array to a new array for resizing. The ArrayList is part of the java.util package.

Iterating Over a Collection

```
// For a set or list
// collection is the set or list object
for (Iterator it=collection.iterator();
      it.hasNext(); ) {
    Object element = it.next();
}

// For keys of a map
for (Iterator it =map.keySet().iterator();
     it.hasNext(); ) {
    Object key = it.next();
}

// For values of a map
for (Iterator it =map.values().iterator();
     it.hasNext(); ) {
    Object value = it.next();
}

// For both the keys and values of a map
for (Iterator it =map.entrySet().iterator();
     it.hasNext(); ) {
    Map.Entry entry = (Map.Entry)it.next();
    Object key = entry.getKey();
    Object value = entry.getValue();
}
```

The java.util package contains an Iterator class that makes iterating over a collection a relatively simple task. To iterate over a collection object, you first obtain an Iterator object by calling the iterator() method on the collection object. Once you have the Iterator object, you can step though it using the next() method. The next() method will return the next item in the collection. Because the next() method returns a generic Object type, you should cast the return value to be the type you are expecting. Using the hasNext() method, you can check to see if there are additional elements that have not yet been processed. This makes it convenient to create a "for" loop as shown in this phrase to step through all the elements in a collection.

In the previous phrase, we show how to iterate over a set or list, the keys of a map, the values of a map, and both keys and values of a map.

NOTE: You might want to use iterators to expose collections through APIs. The advantage of exposing the data through an iterator is that the calling code does not have to know or care about how the data is stored. With this implementation, you could change the collection type without having to change the API.

Creating a Mapped Collection

```
HashMap map = new HashMap();
map.put(key1, obj1);
map.put(key2, obj2);
map.get(key3, obj3);
```

In this phrase, we use a HashMap to create a mapped collection of objects. The HashMap has a put() method that accepts two parameters. The first parameter is a key value, and the second parameter is the object you want to store in the map. So, in this phrase, we are storing three objects—`obj1`, `obj2`, and `obj3`—indexed by keys—`key1`, `key2`, and `key3`, respectively. The `HashMap` class is one of the most commonly used Java classes. In a `HashMap`, the objects put into a map should all be of the same class type. So if `obj1` is a `String` object, then `obj2` and `obj3` should also be `String` objects.

To retrieve the objects that you put into the collection, you use the `get()` method of the `HashMap`. The `get()` method takes a single parameter, which is the key of the element you want to retrieve. If the element is found, it will be returned as a generic `Object`, so you would want to cast it to the type you are expecting. If the element you are trying to retrieve does not exist, a null value is returned.

NOTE: JDK 1.5 introduces a new language feature called Generics which would allow you to retrieve items from a HashMap without having to do any casting. Sun makes available an excellent article on using Generics at this site: http://java.sun.com/developer/technicalArticles/J2SE/generics/index.html

---

It is important that objects you are using as key values in a `HashMap` implement the `equals()` and `hashCode()` methods. These methods are used by the `HashMap` implementation to find elements in the map. If an object used as a key value does not have these methods implemented, key objects will be matched by their identity only, meaning that to find a matching key, you'd have to pass in the identical object instance when trying to retrieve an object. This is usually not what you want.

Sorting a Collection

```
// sorting an array
int[] myInts = {1,5,7,8,2,3};
Arrays.sort(myInts);

// sorting a List
List myList = new ArrayList();
myList.put(obj1);
myList.put(obj2);
Collections.sort(myList);
```

The `Arrays` class is a class in the `java.util` package that contains a bunch of static methods for manipulating arrays. The useful method here is the `sort()` method. The `sort()` method takes an array of objects or primitives along with optional from and to indexes. The from index, if passed, would specify the index of the first element to be sorted, and the to index would specify the index of the last element to be sorted. Primitives are sorted in ascending order. When using this method to sort objects, all the objects must implement the `Comparable` interface, or alternatively a `Comparator` object can be passed. In our phrase, we have an array of integers of type int. We pass this array to the `Arrays.sort()` method, and the array is sorted. It is important to point out that the actual array that is passed in is the array that is sorted and thus modified. A new sorted array is not returned. The `sort()` method has a void return type.

The `Collections` class is another class in the `java.util` package, which contains static methods that operate on other collection objects. The `sort()` method takes a

List object as input and sorts the items in the list into ascending order, according to natural ordering of the elements. Similar to the sort() method in the Arrays object, all elements in the List passed into this method must implement the Comparable interface, or alternatively a Comparator object can be passed along with the List. The list passed into the sort() method is modified. In the second part of our phrase, we create an ArrayList object and use the Collections.sort() method to sort it. In this example, since no Comparator object was passed in, the objects obj1 and obj2 must have implemented the Comparable interface.

If the default sort order is not what you want, you can implement the Comparator interface to define your own sorting mechanism. The comparator that you define can then be passed as the second argument to the sort() method of either Collections or Arrays class.

In addition to the classes described, the Collections Framework contains classes that are inherently sorted such as the TreeSet and TreeMap. If you use these classes, the elements are automatically sorted when they are placed into the collection. For a TreeSet, the elements are sorted in ascending order according to the Comparable interface or by the Comparator provided at creation time. For a TreeMap, the elements are in ascending key order according to the Comparable interface or by the Comparator provided at creation time.

Finding an Object in a Collection

```
// finding an object in an ArrayList
int index = myArrayList.indexOf(myStringObj);

// finding an object by value in a HashMap
myHashMap.containsValue(myStringObj);
// finding an object by key in a HashMap
myHashMap.containsKey(myStringObj);
```

The examples shown in this phrase illustrate how you can find objects in the most commonly used collections—the `ArrayList`, and the `HashMap`. Using the `indexOf()` method of the `ArrayList`, you are able to find the position in the array where a given object is located. If the object passed into the `indexOf()` method is not found, a value of `-1` is returned. A `HashMap` indexes items by objects instead of by integer values as an `ArrayList` does. You can use the `containsValue()` or `containsKey()` methods to determine if a `HashMap` contains the passed in object as either a value or a key in the map. The `containsValue()` and `containsKey()` methods will return a boolean value.

Some additional methods for finding objects in collections are the `binarySearch()` and `contains()` methods.

The `binarySearch()` method is a method in the utility classes `Arrays` and `Collections`. This method searches an array using the binary search algorithm. Prior to calling the `binarySearch()` method of the `Arrays` class, the array must be sorted. If it is not sorted, the results will be undefined. The sorting of the array can be done using the `Arrays.sort()` method. If an array contains multiple items with the value specified as the search value, there is no guarantee which one will be found. Likewise, the `binarySearch()` method in the `Collections` class should only be used on a collection that is sorted into ascending order according to the natural ordering of its elements. This can be done using the `Collections.sort()` method. As with arrays, using this method on an unsorted collection will yield undefined results. If there are multiple elements equal to the object being searched for, there is no guarantee which one will be found.

If a collection is not already sorted, it is probably better to use the `indexOf()` method rather than performing the `sort()` followed by the `binarySearch()`. The `sort()` can be an expensive operation depending on your collection.

Here we use the `binarySearch()` method to search an array of integers:

```
int[] myInts = new int[]{7, 5, 1, 3, 6, 8, 9, 2};
Arrays.sort(myInts);
int index = Arrays.binarySearch(myInts, 6);
System.out.println("Value 6 is at index: " + index);
```

This will result in an output of

```
The value 6 is at index 4.
```

The `ArrayList` class also has a `contains()` method that can be used to check if a given object is a member of a given `ArrayList`.

Converting a Collection to an Array

```
// converting an ArrayList into an array of objects
Object[] objects = aArrayList.toArray();

// converting a HashMap into an array of objects
Object[] mapObjects = aHashMap.entrySet().toArray();
```

As you can see in this phrase, it is a relatively simple task in Java to convert a collection, such as an `ArrayList` or `HashMap`, into a regular array of objects. The `ArrayList` has a `toArray()` method that returns an array of objects. Converting a HashMap to an array is slightly different. First, we must get the values stored in the `HashMap` as an array, using the `entrySet()` method. The `entrySet()` method returns us the data values as a Java `Set`. Once we have the `Set` object, we can call the `toArray()` method to get an array containing the values that were stored in the `HashMap`.

5

Dates and Times

Most Java programs have to deal with dates and times at one point or another. Fortunately, Java has good built-in support for working with dates and times. Three primary classes are used in most Java programs to store and manipulate times and dates. Those classes are the `java.util.Date` class, the `java.sql.Date` class, and the `java.util.Calendar` class.

Many of the methods in the `java.util.Date` class have become deprecated, meaning that you should avoid using them in new development. The deprecated methods generally deal with the creation and manipulation of dates. For these operations, the `java.util.Calendar` class is the preferred mechanism to use. It is also easy to convert between `Date` and `Calendar` objects, so if you prefer to pass your dates around as `Date` objects, you can still avoid using the deprecated methods. You would simply convert the dates to `Calendar` objects when it's time to manipulate the dates. A phrase in this chapter shows you how to convert between `Date` and `Calendar` objects.

Finding Today's Date

```
Date today = new java.util.Date();
System.out.println("Today's Date is " +
     today.toString());
```

The Date object in the java.util package is a class that you should be familiar with if your program deals with dates and times, as it is commonly used. Getting the current time and date is a very simple task. When you create an instance of the Date object, it is initialized with the current time and date.

An alternative method to getting the current date and time is to use the Calendar class. The following code will also get you the current date and time:

```
Calendar cal = Calendar.getInstance();
```

This will produce a Calendar object, cal, initialized with the current date and time.

Converting Between Date and Calendar Objects

```
// Date to Calendar conversion
Date myDate = new java.util.Date();
Calendar myCal = Calendar.getInstance();
myCal.setTime(myDate);

// Calendar to Date conversion
Calendar newCal = Calendar.getInstance();
Date newDate = newCal.getTime();
```

If you're working with times and dates, you'll often find it necessary to convert between java Date and Calendar objects. Fortunately, as shown in the phrase, this is a very simple thing to do. A Calendar object has a `setTime()` method that takes a `java.util.Date` object as a parameter and sets the `Calendar` object to the date and time contained in the `Date` object passed in. To convert in the opposite direction, you can use the `getTime()` method of the `Calendar` class, which returns the date and time of the calendar as a `java.util.Date` object.

In most Java applications, you'll find uses of both the `Date` and `Calendar` classes; thus knowing how to convert from one to the other is something you want to be familiar with. I'd recommend that you create utility methods to perform these conversions so that you can convert from any place in your code with a simple method call. For example, below we show simple methods for converting from a `Calendar` to a `Date` class, and a `Date` to a `Calendar` class:

```
public static Date calToDate(Calendar cal) {
    return cal.getTime();
}

public static Calendar dateToCal(Date date) {
    Calendar myCal = Calendar.getInstance();
    myCal.setTime(date);
    return myCal;
}
```

Printing Date/Time in a Given Format

```
Date todaysDate = new java.util.Date();
SimpleDateFormat formatter =
  new SimpleDateFormat("EEE, dd MMM yyyy HH:mm:ss");
String formattedDate = formatter.format(todaysDate);
System.out.println("Today's Date and Time is: "
  + formattedDate);
```

Java contains formatting classes that can be used to format a date into a desired format. The most commonly used class for formatting dates is the `SimpleDateFormat` class. This class takes a format string as input to its constructor and returns a format object that can then be used to format `Date` objects. Calling the `format()` method of the `SimpleDateFormat` object will return a string that contains the formatted representation of the `Date` that is passed into the method as a parameter.

The output of the phrase shown will be the following:

```
Today's Date and Time is: Mon, 27 Feb 2006 11:18:33
```

The formatting string passed to the `SimpleDateFormat` constructor can be a bit cryptic to read if you don't know the formatting codes to use. Table 5.1 shows the formatting codes that can be passed into the `SimpleDateFormat` constructor. In our phrase, we used the following formatting string:

```
"EEE, dd MMM yyyy HH:mm:ss"
```

Referring to Table 5.1, let's break down this format string to understand what we are asking for.

```
EEE  = 3 character representation of the day of the
       week. (i.e. Tue)
, = puts a comma in the output.
dd = 2 character representation of the day of the
     month. (i.e. 1 - 31)
MMM = 3 character representation of the month of
      the year. (i.e. Feb)
yyyy = 4 digit year string. (i.e. 2006)
HH:mm:ss = The hour minute and seconds separated by
           semi-colons. (i.e. 11:18:33)
```

When we put this all together, we get the date string of

```
Mon, 27 Feb 2006 11:18:33
```

Table 5.1 Time and Date Format Codes

Letter	Date or Time Component	Presentation	Examples
G	Era designator	Text	AD
y	Year	Year	1996; 96
M	Month in year	Month	July; Jul; 07
w	Week in year	Number	27
W	Week in month	Number	2
D	Day in year	Number	189
d	Day in month	Number	10
F	Day of week in month	Number	2
E	Day in week	Text	Tuesday; Tue
a	Am/pm marker	Text	PM
H	Hour in day (0-23)	Number	0
k	Hour in day (1-24)	Number	24
K	Hour in am/pm (0-11)	Number	0
h	Hour in am/pm (1-12)	Number	12
m	Minute in hour	Number	30
s	Second in minute	Number	55
S	Millisecond	Number	978
z	Time zone	General time zone	Pacific Standard Time; PST; GMT-08:00
Z	Time zone	RFC 822 time zone	-0800

In addition to creating your own date formatting strings, you can use one of several predefined format strings by using the `getTimeInstance()`, `getDateInstance()`, or `getDateTimeInstance()` methods of the `DateFormat` class. For example, the following code will return a formatter object that will use a date format for your default locale:

```
DateFormat df = DateFormat.getDateInstance();
```

The `df` formatter can then be used in the same way we used the `SimpleDateFormat` object in the phrase. See the JavaDoc available for the `DateFormat` class for a complete discussion of the available standard date/time formatting objects at http://java.sun.com/j2se/1.5.0/docs/api/java/text/DateFormat.html.

Parsing Strings into Dates

```
String dateString = "January 12, 1952 or 3:30:32pm";
DateFormat df = DateFormat.getDateInstance();
Date date = df.parse(dateString);
```

The `DateFormat` object is used to parse a `String` and obtain a `java.util.Date` object. Getting a `DateFormat` object using the `getDateInstance()` method will create a `DateFormat` object using the normal date format for your country. You can then use the `parse()` method of the returned `DateFormat` object to parse a date string into a `Date` object, as shown in the phrase.

The `parse()` method will also accept a second parameter. The second parameter specifies a parse position in the string to be parsed. This specifies a starting point in the string to begin the parsing at.

The java.sql.Date, java.sql.Time, and java.sql.Timestamp classes contain a static method called valueOf() which can also be used to parse simple date strings of the format: "yyyy-mm-dd". This is very useful for converting dates you might use in SQL strings while using JDBC, into Date objects.

These are useful techniques for converting user input date data into Java Date objects for further processing in your application. Your view can return user entered dates as strings, and using this technique, you can convert them to Date objects.

Adding to or Subtracting from a Date or Calendar

```
// date arithmetic using Date objects
Date date = new Date();
long time = date.getTime();
time += 5*24*60*60*1000;
Date futureDate = new Date(time);

// date arithmetic using Calendar objects
Calendar nowCal = Calendar.getInstance();
nowCal.add(Calendar.DATE, 5);
```

If you are using a Date object, the technique for adding or subtracting dates is to first convert the object to a long value using the getTime() method of the Date object. The getTime() method returns the time as measured in milliseconds since the epoch (January 1, 1970, 00:00:00 GMT). You then perform the arithmetic on the long values, and finally convert back to date objects. In the phrase shown, we are adding 5 days to the date object. We convert the 5 days to milliseconds by multiplying by the number of hours in a day

(24), the number of minutes in an hour (60), the number of seconds in a minute (60), and finally by 1,000 to convert from seconds to milliseconds.

You can perform date arithmetic directly on `Calendar` objects using the `add()` method. The `add()` method accepts two parameters, a field, and an amount, both `int` parameters. The quantity specified in the amount field is added to the field specified in the field parameter. The field could be any valid date field, such as day, week, month, year, etc. To subtract time, you would set the amount value to be a negative number. By setting the field parameter to the appropriate `Calendar` constant, you can directly add or subtract days, weeks, months, years, and so on. In the second part of our phrase, we show how to add 5 days to a `Calendar` object.

Calculating the Difference Between Two Dates

```
long time1 = date1.getTime();
long time2 = date2.getTime();
long diff = time2 - time1;
System.out.println("Difference in days = "
    + diff/(1000*60*60*24));
```

This phrase converts two date objects, `date1` and `date2`, into milliseconds—each represented as a `long`. The difference is calculated by subtracting `time1` from `time2`. We then print out the calculated difference in days by performing the arithmetic necessary to convert the millisecond difference into days difference.

Many times, you will want to know the time difference between two dates. A good example of this is in calculating how many days are left before an item is set to expire. If you have the expiration date of an item, you can calculate the days until expiration by calculating the difference between the expiration date and the current date. Below, we show an example of a simple method for making this calculation:

```
public static void daysTillExpired(Date expDate) {
    Date currentDate = new Date();
    long expTime = expDate.getTime();
    long currTime = currentDate.getTime();
    long diff = expTime - currTime;
    return diff/(1000*60*60*24);
}
```

This method takes an expiration date as input, and calculates the number of days until the expiration date is reached. This value in days is returned from the method. This could be a negative number if the expiration date is in the past.

Comparing Dates

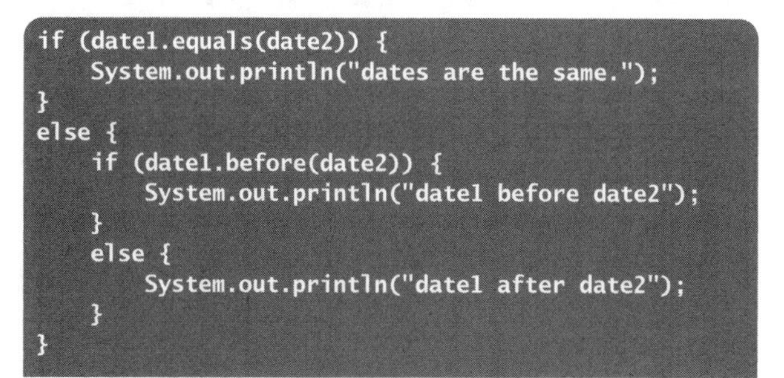

```
if (date1.equals(date2)) {
    System.out.println("dates are the same.");
}
else {
    if (date1.before(date2)) {
        System.out.println("date1 before date2");
    }
    else {
        System.out.println("date1 after date2");
    }
}
```

In this phrase, we make use of the `equals()` and `before()` methods of the `Date` class. The `equals()` method will return true if the data values are the same;

otherwise it will return false. The dates must be the same down to the millisecond in order for the `equals()` method to return true. The `before()` method returns true if the date on which it is called occurs before the date passed as a parameter to this method.

The `Date` class also has an `after()` method, which is used similarly to the `before()` method to determine if the date on which it is called occurs after the date passed in as a parameter.

Another useful method for comparing two dates is the `compareTo()` method of the `Date` class. The `compareTo()` method accepts a date argument and returns an integer value. A value of `0` is returned if the date on which it is called is equal to the date argument. A value less than `0` is returned if the date on which the method is called occurs before the date argument, and a value greater than `0` if the date occurs after the date argument.

Finding the Day of Week/Month/Year or Week Number

```
Calendar cal = Calendar.getInstance();
System.out.println("Day of week: " +
        cal.get(Calendar.DAY_OF_WEEK));
System.out.println("Month: " +
        cal.get(Calendar.MONTH));
System.out.println("Year: " +
        cal.get(Calendar.YEAR));
System.out.println("Week number: " +
        cal.get(Calendar.WEEK_OF_YEAR));
```

You can easily determine values such as the day of the week, the month, the year, the week number, and more using the Calendar object's get() method. In this phrase, we get a Calendar object representing the current date and time using the getInstance() method. We then print out the day of the week, the month, the year, and the week of the year by using the get() method and passing the appropriate Calendar constant to specify the field we want to get.

If you have a Date object and want to get these values, you could convert the Date object to a Calendar object by using the setTime() method of a Calendar instance and passing in the Date object you want to convert. This is shown in the converting between date and calendar objects phrase earlier in this chapter.

Calculating Elapsed Time

```
long start = System.currentTimeMillis();
// do some other stuff…
long end = System.currentTimeMillis();
long elapsedTime = end - start;
```

By calculating elapsed time, we can determine how long it takes to do something or how long a process takes to complete. To do this, we use the System.currentTimeMillis() method to obtain the current time in milliseconds. We use this method at the start and end of the task we want to get the elapsed time for, and then take the difference in times. The actual value that is returned by the System.currentTimeMillis() method is the time since Janauary 1, 00:00:00, 1970 in milliseconds.

JDK 1.5 adds a nanoTime() method to the System class, which allows you to get even more precise timing, down to nanoseconds. In reality, not all platforms support nanosecond resolution, so although the `nanoTime()` method may be available, you can't always count on getting nanosecond resolution.

This is often useful for testing, profiling, and performance monitoring.

6

Pattern Matching with Regular Expressions

Regular expression support was introduced in Java JDK 1.4. Regular expressions specify patterns that can be matched within character sequences. Regular expressions are extremely useful in parsing strings, and will often save a programmer a lot of time and effort in performing a task in comparison to a solution that does not make use of regular expressions. Prior to being added to Java, regular expressions had been used for years by UNIX programmers. Standard UNIX tools such as Sed and Awk make use of regular expressions. Regular expressions are also commonly used in the Perl programming language. The addition of regular expressions to the JDK is a powerful addition to core Java capability.

In this chapter, you will learn how to use the regular expression features of Java to find, match, and replace text. With this knowledge you will be able to identify areas where you can add regular expression processing to your applications.

Regular Expressions in Java

The Java classes you will use to perform regular expression operations are contained in the `java.util.regex` package. The classes are the `Matcher` and the `Pattern` classes. These classes allow you to both find and match character sequences against regular expression patterns. You might be wondering what the difference is between finding and matching. The find operation allows you to find matches in a string, and the match operation requires the entire string to be an exact match of the regular expression. Tasks for which you might have used the `StringTokenizer` class in the past are usually good candidates for exploring the possibility of simplifying your programming with regular expressions.

NOTE: If you are not able to use a version of Java that contains the regular expression package (>= 1.4), a good alternative regular expression package available is the Apache Jakarta Regular Expression package. This book does not cover the Jakarta package, but you can find information and complete documentation for it at http://jakarta.apache.org/regexp.

Table 6.1 shows the common regular expression matching characters. You might want to refer back to this table as you read the phrases in this chapter.

Table 6.1 **Regular Expressions Table—Commonly Used Special Characters**

Special Character	Description
^	Beginning of the string.
$	End of the string.

Table 6.1 **Continued**

Special Character	Description
?	0 or 1 times (refers to the previous expression).
*	0 or more times (refers to the previous expression).
+	1 or more times (refers to the previous expression).
[...]	Alternative characters.
|	Alternative patterns.
.	Any character.
\d	A digit.
\D	A non-digit.
\s	A whitespace character (space, tab, newline, form-feed, carriage return).
\S	A non-whitespace character.
\w	A word character [a-zA-Z_0-9].
\W	A non-word character [^\w].

Notice that although the regular expression escape characters are shown in Table 6.1 as being preceded by a single backslash, when used in a Java string, they must contain two backslashes. This is because in a Java string, the backslash character has special meaning; thus a double backslash escapes the backslash character and is the equivalent of a single backslash character.

A more complete listing of regular expression characters can be found in the JavaDoc for the Pattern class. This is available at this URL http://java.sun.com/j2se/1.5.0/docs/api/java/util/regex/Pattern.html.

Finding Matching Text Using a Regular Expression

```
String pattern = "[TJ]im";
Pattern regPat = Pattern.compile(pattern);
String text = "This is jim and Timothy.";
Matcher matcher = regPat.matcher(text);
if (matcher.find()) {
   String matchedText = matcher.group();
}
```

In this pattern, we make use of the `Pattern` and the `Matcher` classes. We use the static `compile()` method of the `Pattern` class to compile a pattern string into a `Pattern` object. Once we have the `regPat Pattern` object, we use the `matcher()` method, passing in the text string we want to match against. The `matcher()` method returns an instance of the `Matcher` class. Finally, we call the `group()` method of the `Matcher` class to obtain the matched text. The matched text in this phrase will be the character string `"Tim"`. Note that the string `"jim"` will not match because regular expressions are case sensitive by default. To perform a non-case sensitive search, we could slightly modify the code as shown here:

```
String patt = "[TJ]im";
Pattern regPat =
   Pattern.compile(patt, Pattern.CASE_INSENSITIVE);
String text = "This is jim and Timothy.";
Matcher matcher = regPat.matcher(text);
if (matcher.find()) {
   String matchedText = matcher.group();
}
```

This matched text in this code will now be the character string "jim". Because the match is now non-case sensitive, the first match "jim" occurs before the match on "Tim".

Notice that the only difference in this example from our original phrase is that we've added an additional parameter to the compile() method when creating our Pattern object. Here, we pass the CASE_INSENSITIVE flag to denote that we want matching to be performed as non-case sensitive. When we do not include this flag, the default behavior is to perform case sensitive matching.

If your code is required to run in different locales, you would also want to pass the Unicode case flag. So the compile line would look like this in that case:

```
Pattern regPat =
   Pattern.compile(pattern,
                   Pattern.CASE_INSENSITIVE |
                   Pattern.UNICODE_CASE);
```

Notice how we pass multiple flags to the compile() method by logically ORing them together. Pattern flags must be passed at the time the Pattern is first created using the compile() method. Once a Pattern object is created, it is immutable—meaning that it cannot be changed in any way.

In our examples so far, we've used the find() method of the Matcher class to find the first match in our input string. The find() method can be called repeatedly to return successive matches in the input string. The find() method will return true as long as a match is found. It will return false when it does not find a match. If you call find() again after having returned false, it will reset and find the first match again. There is an alternative find() method that takes an int parameter specifying an index from which to start a search from. In all other ways, this find() method behaves identically to the find() method without parameters.

There is also an alternative for getting the match result. We've been using the method group() on the Matcher class. There are also useful methods named start() and end(). The start() method will return the index at the beginning of the previous match. Then the end() method will return the index after the last character matched.

Replacing Matched Text

```
String pattern = "[TJ]im";
Pattern regPat = Pattern.compile(pattern);
String text = "This is jim and Tim.";
Matcher matcher = regPat.matcher(text);
String string2 = matcher.replaceAll("John");
```

In this phrase, we replace text that is matched against our pattern sting with alternate text. The value of string2 at the end of this phrase will be the string

```
This is jim and John.
```

The occurrence of "jim" will not be replaced because the regular expression matching is case sensitive by default. See the previous phrase for non-case sensitive matching. As in basic matching shown in the previous phrase, we use the Pattern, and Matcher classes in the same way. The new step here is our call to the Matcher's replaceAll() method. We pass the text we want to use as replacement text as a parameter. This text will then replace all occurrences of the matched pattern. This is a powerful tool for replacing portions of a string with an alternate string.

Another useful method of replacing text is through the use of the appendReplacement() and appendTail() methods of the Matcher class. Using these methods together allows you to replace occurances of a substring within a string. The code below shows an example of this technique:

```
Pattern p = Pattern.compile("My");
Matcher m = p.matcher("My dad and My mom");
StringBuffer sb = new StringBuffer();
boolean found = m.find();
while(found) {
   m.appendReplacement(sb, "Our");
   found = m.find();
}
m.appendTail(sb);
System.out.println(sb);
```

The output of this code is the following line printed from the System.out.println() method:

```
Our dad and Our mom
```

In this code, we create a Pattern object to match the text "My". The appendReplacement() method writes characters from the input sequence ("My dad and my mom") to the string buffer sb, up to the last character preceding the previous match. It then appends the replacement string, passed as the second parameter, to the string buffer. Finally, it sets the current string position to be at the end of the last match. This repeats as long as matches are found. When no more matches are found, the appendTail() method is used to append the remaining portion of the input sequence to the string buffer.

Finding All Occurrences of a Pattern

```
String pattern = "\\st(\\w)*o(\\w)*";
Pattern regPat = Pattern.compile(pattern);
String text =
   "The words are town tom ton toon house.";
Matcher matcher = regPat.matcher(text);
while (matcher.find()) {
   String matchedText = matcher.group();
   System.out.println("match - " + matchedText);
}
```

In the previous phrases in this chapter, we found a single match of a pattern. In this phrase, we find all the occurrences of a given match pattern that occurs within a string. The pattern we use for this phrase is `"\\st(\\w)*o(\\w)*"`. This regular expression will find any words that begin with `t` and contain the letter `o` in them. The output printed from our `System.out.println()`statements will be the following:

```
town
tom
ton
toon
```

Here we break down this regular expression and show what each element gives us:

```
\\s  Special regular expression character
     matching a whitespace character.
t  this matches the letter t.
\\w*  Special regular expression character matching
```

```
     zero or more word characters (non-whitespace).
o  this matches the leter o.
\\w*  Special regular expression character matching
      zero or more word characters (non-whitespace).
```

This regular expression would not match the first word of the string even if it started with a `t` and contained an `o`. This is because the first piece of the regular expression matches on a whitespace character, and typically the string will not start with a whitespace character.

Printing Lines Containing a Pattern

```
String pattern = "^a";
Pattern regPat = Pattern.compile(pattern);
Matcher matcher = regPat.matcher("");
BufferedReader reader =
   new BufferedReader(new FileReader("file.txt"));
String line;
while ((line = reader.readLine()) != null) {
    matcher.reset(line);
    if (matcher.find()) {
         System.out.println(line);
    }
}
```

This phrase demonstrates how we might search through a file to find all the lines that contain a given pattern. Here we use the `BufferedReader` class to read lines from a text file. We attempt to match each line against our pattern using the `find()` method of the `Matcher` class. The `find()` method will return true if the pattern is found within the line passed as its parameter. We print all the lines that match the given pattern. Note that this piece of code can throw `FileNotFoundException` and `IOException`, and these would need to be handled in your real code. In this phrase, the regular expression would match any lines contained in our input file that start with the lowercase letter `a`.

The regular expression pattern we use is broken down as follows:

```
^  Special regular expression character
   matching the beginning of a string.
a  matches the character letter a.
```

Matching Newlines in Text

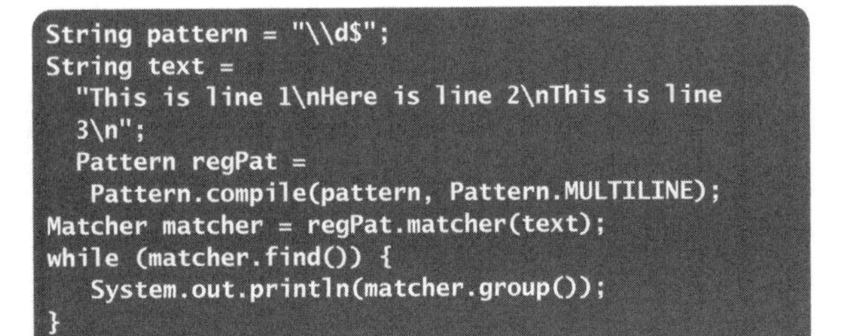

```
String pattern = "\\d$";
String text =
  "This is line 1\nHere is line 2\nThis is line
  3\n";
  Pattern regPat =
   Pattern.compile(pattern, Pattern.MULTILINE);
Matcher matcher = regPat.matcher(text);
while (matcher.find()) {
   System.out.println(matcher.group());
}
```

In this phrase, we use the `Pattern.MULTILINE` flag to match newlines in a text string. By default, the regular expression characters `^` and `$` only match the beginning and end of an entire string. So, if a string contained multiple lines, distinguished with newline characters, the `^` expression would still only match the beginning of the string by default. If we pass the `Pattern.MULTILINE` flag to the `Pattern.compile()` method as we do in this phrase, the `^` will now match the first character following a line terminator, and the

$ will match just before the line terminator. So, by using the Pattern.MULTILINE flag, the ^ would now match the start of every line in a string containing multiple lines separating by newline characters.

The output of this phrase will be

```
1
2
3
```

We use the pattern "\\d$". In this regular expression, the \\d matches any single digit. Because we are in MULTILINE mode, the $ matches just before a line terminator. So, the net effect is that our regular expression will match the single digit character contained at the end of any line. Thus, we get the output shown previously.

7

Numbers

Working with numbers in Java is a subject that every programmer should become proficient in, as nearly every program deals with numbers of one form or another. In this chapter, we primarily use the basic numeric Java types, their object wrappers, and the `java.lang.Math` class.

Table 7.1 summarizes the built-in types that Java offers and lists their wrapper objects available. Note that the boolean type does not have a bit size because it can contain only two discrete values, a value of true or false.

Table 7.1 **Java's Built-In Types**

Type	Size in bits	Wrapper Object
byte	8	Byte
short	16	Short
int	32	Integer
long	64	Long
float	32	Float
double	64	Double
char	16	Character
boolean	--	Boolean

The object wrapper classes are useful when you want to treat a basic type like an object. For example, this might be useful if you want to define an API in terms of objects only. When wrapped as objects, the basic types can also be serialized.

Checking Whether a String Is a Valid Number

```
try {
    int result = Integer.parseInt(aString);
}
catch (NumberFormatException ex) {
   System.out.println(
      "The string does not contain a valid
      number.");
}
```

In this phrase, we use the `parseInt()` static method of the `Integer` class to attempt to convert the string parameter into an integer. If the string parameter cannot be converted into a valid integer, the `NumberFormatException` is thrown. Therefore, if we do not get a `NumberFormatException`, we can safely assume that the `parseInt()` method was able to parse the string into an integer value.

You may want to consider declaring the `int` variable outside of the try block so that if the `NumberFormatException` is thrown, you can assign a default value to the variable in the catch block. The code for this technique would be as follows:

```
int result = 0;
try {
    result = Integer.parseInt(aString);
}
```

```
catch (NumberFormatException ex) {
   result = DEFAULT_VALUE;
}
```

Comparing Floating Point Numbers

```
Float a = new Float(3.0f);
Float b = new Float(3.0f);
if (a.equals(b)) {
  // they are equal
}
```

Because of rounding errors that can occur when working with floating point numbers, you have to be a bit more careful when trying to compare them. Therefore, instead of comparing the basic Java floating point types of `float` and `double` using the == operator; you should instead compare their object equivalents. The `equals()` method on `Float` and `Double` will return true only if the two values are exactly the same, bit for bit, or if they are both the value `NaN`. The value `NaN` stands for not a number. This value indicates a value that is not a valid number.

In the real world, when comparing floating point numbers, you might not want to compare for an exact match, but within an acceptable difference range. This acceptable range is usually referred to as a *tolerance*. Unfortunately, there is no built-in capability to do this using the Java standard classes or types, but you could fairly easily create your own `equals()` method to achieve this. Here we show some code that you could use to create such a method:

```
float f1 = 2.99f;
float f2 = 3.00f;
float tolerance = 0.05f;
if (f1 == f2) System.out.println("they are equal");
else {
   if (Math.abs(f1-f2) < tolerance) {
      System.out.println("within tolerance");
   }
}
```

We first compare the floating point numbers using the == operator. If they are identically equal, we print an appropriate message. If they are not equal, we check to see if the absolute value of their difference is less than the desired tolerance value. Using this technique, you could create a useful method that would take two floating point values and a tolerance, and return a result indicating whether the values are equal within the tolerance range.

Rounding Floating Point Numbers

```
// rounding a double value
long longResult = Math.round(doubleValue);
// rounding a float value
int intResult = Math.round(floatValue);
```

If you want to convert a floating point number to an integer, you have to be careful. If you simply cast the floating point number to an `int` or `long`, Java will convert it to an `int` or `long` by just truncating the decimal portion. So even if you had a value such as 20.99999, you'd end up with 20 after casting it to an `int` or `long` value. The proper way to perform floating point number to integer conversion is to use the Math.round() method. In this phrase, we show how to round a double value and a float value. If you pass a double value to the Math.round() method, a long result is returned. If you pass a float value to the Math.round() method, an int result is returned. The Math.round() method will round a value up if the decimal portion of the floating point number is 0.5 or greater, and it will be rounded down for decimal numbers less than 0.5.

Formatting Numbers

```
double value = 1623542.765;
NumberFormat numberFormatter;
String formattedValue;
numberFormatter = NumberFormat.getNumberInstance();
formattedValue = numberFormatter.format(value);
System.out.format("%s%n", formattedValue);
```

In most applications, there is a need to display numbers. Fortunately, Java has built-in support for formatting numbers so that they will look as you want them to when you display them in your application.

This phrase will generate the following formatted number as output:

```
1,623,542.765
```

In this phrase, we use the NumberFormat class to format a double value into a comma separated string representation of its value. The NumberFormat class is found in the java.text package and is also very useful for code that you will internationalize. The NumberFormat class supports the formatting of numbers and currency, and it also knows how to represent numbers and currency in different locales.

The `NumberFormat` class can also be used to easily format percent values for display. Here, we show how you can use the `NumberFormat` class to format a percent for display:

```
double percent = 0.80;
NumberFormat percentFormatter;
String formattedPercent;
percentFormatter =
NumberFormat.getPercentInstance();
formattedPercent = percentFormatter.format(percent);
System.out.format("%s%n", formattedPercent);
```

The output of this code will be

```
80%
```

The `NumberFormat` class also has a `parse()` method that you can use to parse strings containing numbers into a `Number` object, from which you can get a numeric type.

JDK1.5 introduced a `java.util.Formatter` class, which is a general-purpose formatting object that can format a wide variety of types. In addition to numbers, this class can also format dates and times. This class is documented very well in the JDK1.5 documentation at http://java.sun.com/j2se/1.5.0/docs/api/java/util/Formatter.html.

JDK1.5 also added two utility methods to the `java.io.PrintStream` class for easy formatting of an `OutputStream`. The new methods are the `format()` and `printf()` methods. Both of these methods take a format string and a variable number of `Object` arguments as input parameters. These methods are very similar to the traditional `printf` and `scanf` methods of formatting strings in the C language. For details on using these methods, refer to the JDK1.5 documentation at http://java.sun.com/j2se/1.5.0/docs/api/java/io/Print Stream.html.

In the next phrase, we show how you can format currency values for display, also using the `NumberFormat` class.

Formatting Currencies

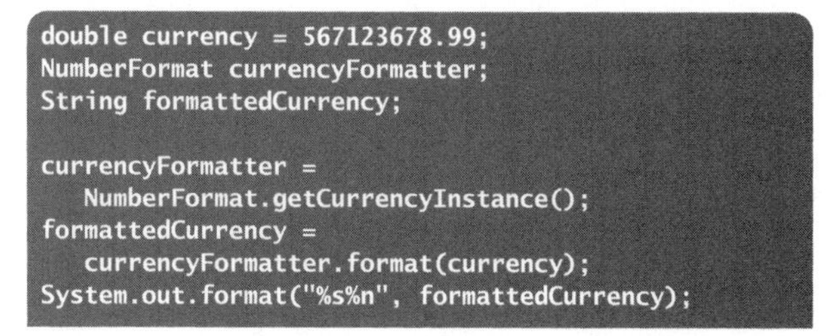

```
double currency = 567123678.99;
NumberFormat currencyFormatter;
String formattedCurrency;

currencyFormatter =
   NumberFormat.getCurrencyInstance();
formattedCurrency =
   currencyFormatter.format(currency);
System.out.format("%s%n", formattedCurrency);
```

As with the previous phrase on formatting numbers, here we make use of the `NumberFormat` class, but this time to format a currency value. We use the `getCurrencyInstance()` of the `NumberFormat` class to get a currency formatting instance of the class. Using this instance, we can pass a floating point value and it will return a formatted currency value. The output of the phrase shown will be the following string:

```
$567,123,678.99
```

In addition to placing commas in the appropriate places, the currency formatter also automatically adds the dollar sign character preceding the string.

Converting an Integer to Binary, Octal, and Hexadecimal

```
int intValue = 24;
String binaryStr = Integer.toBinaryString(intValue);
String octalStr = Integer.toOctalString(intValue);
String hexStr = Integer.toHexString(intValue);
```

Using the `Integer` class, it is easy to convert an integer value from decimal to binary, octal, or hexadecimal. The relevant static methods on the `Integer` class are the `toBinaryString()`, `toOctalString()`, and `toHexString()` methods. In this phrase, we use each of these methods—each time passing in an integer value and getting a `String` returned that contains the integer in binary, octal, and hex format, respectively.

Generating Random Numbers

```
Random rn = new Random();
int value = rn.nextInt();
double dvalue = rn.nextDouble();
```

To generate random numbers, we use the `Random` class found in the `java.util` package. By default, the `Random` class uses the current time of day as a seed value for its random number generator. You can also set a seed value by passing it as a parameter to the constructor of `Random`. The `nextInt()` method will produce a 32-bit integer random number.

An alternate way of generating random numbers is to use the `random()` method of the `Math` class in the `java.lang` package.

```
double value = Math.random();
```

This method will return a double value with a positive sign, greater than or equal to 0.0 and less than 1.0. To generate a value within a specific range, you could add the lower bound to the result of Math.random() and multiply by the range. For example, the following code would give us a random number between 5 and 20:

```
double value = (5+Math.random())*15;
```

The Random class and the random() method of the Math class will actually give you a pseudorandom number, not a true random number. This means that the random number is generated using a mathematical formula and an input seed value. Given the seed value and knowledge of the inner workings of the Random class, it would be possible to predict these random values. Therefore, these classes are probably not the best solution for a random number generator for use in high security applications. For most applications, though, these are perfectly acceptable random number generators.

Calculating Trigonometric Functions

```
// calculating cosine
double cosine = Math.cos(45);
// calculating sine
double sine = Math.sin(45);
// calculating tangent
double tangent = Math.tan(45);
```

The Math class found in the java.lang package has methods for easily calculating all the trigonometric functions. In this phrase, we show how you can easily determine the cosine, sine, and tangent of a given angle. The `Math` class also has methods for calculating the arc cosine, arc sine, and arc tangent, as well as the hyperbolic sine, cosine, and tangent. Each of these methods accepts a single input parameter of double type and returns a result type of double.

Calculating a Logarithm

```
double logValue = Math.log(125.5);
```

In this phrase, we use the `log()` method of the `java.lang.Math` class to calculate the logarithm of the parameter passed in. We pass in a value of `double` type, and the return value is also a `double` value. The `log()` method calculates the natural logarithm, using base e, where e is the standard value of 2.71828.

JDK1.5 added a new method to the `Math` class for directly calculating a base 10 logarithm. This is the `log10()` method. Similar to the `log()` method, this method takes a `double` input parameter, and returns a `double` result type. We can use this method to easily calculate a base 10 logarithm as follows:

```
double logBase10 = Math.log10(200);
```

8

Input and Output

In most cases, input and output is the ultimate goal of an application. An application is only useful if it can spit out results and take in user or machine generated input to process. In this chapter, we cover basic phrases for performing input and output.

The `java.io` and `java.util` packages are home to most of the classes that we will use in this chapter for performing input and output tasks. In this chapter, we will show you how to read and write files, work with zip archives, format your output, and work with the standard operating system streams.

As you read the phrases in this chapter, keep in mind that many of the phrases have the possibility of throwing exceptions such as the `java.io.IOException` in any real program. In the phrases, we do not include exception handling code. In any real application, exception handling is a necessity.

Reading Text from Standard Input

```
BufferedReader inStream = new BufferedReader (
       new InputStreamReader(System.in)
     );
String inLine = "";
while ( !(inLine.equalsIgnoreCase("quit"))) {
    System.out.print("prompt> ");
    inLine = inStream.readLine();
}
```

In a console program, it is common to read from the standard input, typically the command line. In this phrase, we show how you can read the standard input into a Java `String` variable.

Java contains three streams that are connected to the operating system streams. These are the standard input, standard output, and standard error streams. Respectively, they are defined in Java as the streams `System.in`, `System.out`, and `System.err`. We can make use of these streams to read or write to the operating systems standard input and output.

In our phrase, we create a `BufferedReader` to read from the `System.in` stream. Using this reader, we continue to read input lines from the standard input until the user types the word "quit."

Writing to Standard Output

```
System.out.println("Hello, World!");
```

`System.out` is a `PrintStream` that will write output to the standard output. This is typically the console. `System.out` is one of the three streams that Java defines to connect with the standard operating system's streams. The other streams are the `System.in` and the `System.err` streams—for reading from standard input and writing to standard error.

The `System.out` stream is probably the most often used of all the standard operating system streams. `System.out` has been put to use by nearly every programmer to assist with debugging an application. Because this stream writes to the console, it makes a handy tool to see what's going on at a particular point in your application. In general though, `System.out` statements should not be left in a code after initial debugging as they can affect performance of the application. A better long-term strategy for gathering debug information in your application is to make use of a logging facility such as what is available in `java.util.logging`, or the popular Apache Log4J package.

Formatting Output

```
float hits=3;
float ab=10;
String formattedTxt =
   String.format("Batting average: %.3f", hits/ab);
```

In this phrase, we use the `format()` method to format an output string that prints a baseball batting average in the standard format of three decimal places. The batting average is defined as the number of `hits`, divided by the number of at-bats, `ab`. The format specifier `%.3f` tells the formatter to print the average as a floating point number with three digits following the decimal point.

JDK1.5 introduced the `java.util.Formatter` class, which can be used to easily format text. The `Formatter` class works very similar to the `printf` function in the C language, and provides support for layout justification and alignment, common formats for numeric, string, and date/time data, and locale-specific output. An example of using the `Formatter` class directly is shown here:

```
StringBuffer buffer = new StringBuffer();
Formatter formatter = new Formatter(buffer,
Locale.US);
formatter.format("Value of PI: %6.4f", Math.PI);
System.out.println(buffer.toString());
```

The corresponding output:

```
Value of PI: 3.1416
```

In this example, we create a `Formatter` instance and use it to format the value of the standard mathematical value PI. The value of PI contains an infinite amount of decimal places, but you typically want to restrict it to a small number of decimal places when printing it. In this example, we used the format specifier of %6.4f. The value 6 says that the output for this number should be no more than 6 characters wide, including the decimal point. The value 4 indicates that the precision of the decimal value should be 4 decimal places. Thus the value printed is 6 characters in length and has 4 decimal places: 3.1416.

In addition to using the `Formatter` class directly, you can use the `format()` and `printf()` methods of the `System.out` and `System.err` streams. For example, here we print the local time using the `format()` method on the `System.out` stream:

```
System.out.format("Local time: %tT",
                  Calendar.getInstance());
```

This method will print the local time as shown here:

```
Local time: 16:25:14
```

The `String` class also contains a static `format()` method that can be used to directly format strings. We can use this static method, for example, to easily format a date string as we do here:

```
Calendar c =
   ew GregorianCalendar(1999, Calendar.JANUARY, 6);
String s =
   String.format(
         "Timmy's Birthday: %1$tB %1$te, %1$tY", c);
```

This will code create the following formatted `String` value:

```
Timmy's Birthday: January 6, 1999
```

All the methods that produce formatted output that we've discussed take a format string and an argument list as parameters. The format string is a `String` that might contain text and one or more format specifiers. In our birthday formatting example, the format string would be `"Timmy's Birthday: %1$tm %1$te,%1$tY"`. The `%1$tm`, `%1$te`, and `$1$tY` elements are format specifiers. The remainder of the string is static text. These format specifiers indicate how the arguments should be processed and where in the string they should be placed. Referring to our birthday example again, the argument list is just the `Calendar` object `c`. Although in this case, we have only one argument, the argument list might contain multiple items. All parameters passed to the formatting methods after the format string are considered arguments.

Format specifiers have the following format:

```
%[argument_index$][flags][width][.precision]conver-
sion
```

The `argument_index` references an argument in the list of arguments passed to the formatting method. The list is indexed starting at 1. So to reference the first argument, you would use `1$`.

The `flags` element is a set of characters that modify the output format. The set of valid flags depends on the conversion.

The `width` is a nonnegative decimal integer indicating the minimum number of characters to be written to the output.

The `precision` is a nonnegative decimal integer normally used to restrict the number of characters. The specific behavior depends on the conversion.

The `conversion` is a character indicating how the argument should be formatted. The set of valid conversions for a given argument depends on the argument's data type.

All the specifier elements are optional except for the conversion character.

Table 8.1 shows a list of valid conversion characters. For details about date and time conversions, refer to the JavaDoc for the Formatter class at: http://java.sun.com/j2se/1.5.0/docs/api/.

Table 8.1 **Formatter Format Codes**

Code	Description
b	If the argument *arg* is `null`, the result is `"false"`. If *arg* is a `boolean` or `Boolean`, the result is the string returned by `String.valueOf()`. Otherwise, the result is `"true"`.
h	If the argument *arg* is `null`, the result is `"null"`. Otherwise, the result is obtained by invoking `Integer.toHexString(arg.hashCode())`.
s	If the argument *arg* is `null`, the result is `"null"`. If *arg* implements `Formattable`, `arg.formatTo` is invoked. Otherwise, the result is obtained by invoking `arg.toString()`.
c	The result is a Unicode character.
d	The result is formatted as a decimal integer.
o	The result is formatted as an octal integer.
x	The result is formatted as a hexadecimal integer.
f	The result is formatted as a decimal number.
e	The result is formatted as a decimal number in computerized scientific notation.
g	The result is formatted using computerized scientific notation or decimal format, depending on the precision and the value after rounding.
a	The result is formatted as a hexadecimal floating point number with a significand and an exponent.

Table 8.1 Continued

Code	Description
t	Prefix for date and time conversion characters.
n	The result is the platform-specific line separator.
%	The result is a literal '%'.

Refer to the JavaDoc documentation of the `Formatter` class for a complete list of the available format codes. This is available at: http://java.sun.com/j2se/1.5.0/docs/api/java/util/Formatter.html.

Opening a File by Name

```
// opening a file for reading
BufferedReader is =
   new BufferedReader(new FileReader("file.txt"));
// opening a file for writing
BufferedWriter out =
   new BufferedWriter(new FileWriter("afile.txt"));
```

In this phrase, we show how you can create a `BufferedReader` for reading input from a file specified by a filename—in this case `somefile.txt`—and how you can create a `BufferedWriter` for writing text to an output file specified by name, `afile.txt`.

It is very easy to open a file by name in Java. Most of the input and output stream and reader classes you will use have an option of specifying the file by name in the stream or reader's constructor.

Reading a File into a Byte Array

```
File file = new File(fileName);
InputStream is = new FileInputStream(file);
long length = file.length();
byte[] bytes = new byte[(int)length];
int offset = 0;
int numRead = 0;
while ((offset < bytes.length)
         &&
        ((numRead=is.read(bytes,
                          offset,
                          bytes.length-offset))
         >= 0)) {
       offset += numRead;
}
is.close();
```

This phrase will read the file specified by `fileName` into the `bytes` byte array. Notice that the `file.length()` method returns us the length of the file in bytes as a `long` value, but we must use an `int` value to initialize the byte array, so we cast the `long` value to an `int` value. In a real program, you would probably want to be sure that the length value would indeed fit into an `int` type before blindly casting it. Using the `read()` method of the `InputStream`, we continue to read in bytes from the file until either the byte array is filled up, or there are no more bytes to read from the file.

Reading Binary Data

```
InputStream is = new FileInputStream(fileName);
int offset = 0;
int bytesRead =
   is.read(bytes, offset, bytes.length-offset);
```

Using the `read()` method, we can read binary data from a file into an array of bytes. In this phrase, we read from the `is` input stream into the `bytes` byte array. In this phrase, the `bytes` array is assumed to have been previously initialized as a byte array, and the `fileName` variable is the name of a valid file. The `offset` variable points to a starting location in the `bytes` array to begin writing the data to. This is useful when you are in a loop reading data from a file and you don't want to overwrite previous data stored in the byte array. For each iteration through the loop, you would update the offset location. We've seen this in the previous phrase, *Reading a File into a Byte Array*. Here is the relevant code example:

```
while ( (offset < bytes.length)
        &&
        ( (numRead=is.read(bytes, offset,
bytes.length-offset)) >= 0) ) {
       offset += numRead;
}
```

In this code example, we are writing data from the input stream `is` into the `bytes` array. We continue to read from the file until we've either filled up the `bytes` array, or there is no more data to read from the file.

Seeking in a File

```
File file = new File("somefile.bin");
RandomAccessFile raf =
   new RandomAccessFile(file, "rw");
raf.seek(file.length());
```

Using the `seek()` method of the `RandomAccessFile` class, we can seek to any desired position within a file.

In this phrase, we first create a File object, which is then used to create a RandomAccessFile instance. Using the RandomAccessFile instance, raf, we seek to the end of the file by passing in the file.length() value as a parameter to the seek() method.

After using the seek() method to find the desired position within a file, we can then use the read() or write() methods of the RandomAccessFile class to read or write data at that exact position.

Reading a JAR or Zip Archive

```
// reading a zip file
ZipFile file = new ZipFile(filename);
Enumeration entries = file.entries();
while (entries.hasMoreElements()) {
    ZipEntry entry =
(ZipEntry)entries.nextElement();
    if (entry.isDirectory()) {
        // process directory
    }
    else {
        // process file
    }
}
file.close();
```

Java has built-in support for reading and writing Zip archive files. A JAR file is a Zip file that contains specified content, so you can also use the Zip file classes and methods to read a JAR file. The zip classes are contained in the java.util.zip package, which is part of the standard JDK. In this phrase, we first create a ZipFile object by passing the filename of an existing Zip file to the constructor of the ZipFile class. We then get all the Zip file's entries into an enumeration type by calling the entries() method of the ZipFile object. Once we have the Zip file entries as an enumeration, we can step through the entries and instantiate a ZipEntry object for each entry. From the ZipEntry object, we can determine if the particular entry being processed is a directory or a file. Based on that knowledge, we could then process the entry appropriately.

Creating a Zip Archive

```
// writing a zip file
ZipOutputStream out =
   new ZipOutputStream(
         new FileoutputStream(zipFileName));
FileInputStream in = new
FileInputStream(fileToZip1);
out.putNextEntry(new ZipEntry(fileToZip1));
int len;
byte[] buf = new byte[1024];
while ((len = in.read(buf)) > 0) {
    out.write(buf,0,len);
}
out.closeEntry();
in.close();
out.close();
```

In the previous phrase, we showed how you can read from a Zip file. In this phrase, we create a Zip file. To do this, we first construct a ZipOutputStream by passing to its constructor a FileOutputStream object pointing to the file we want to create as our Zip file. We then create a FileInputStream for a file that we want to add to our Zip file. We use the putNextEntry() method of the ZipOutputStream to add the file to our Zip archive. The putNextEntry() method takes a ZipEntry object as input, so we must construct the ZipEntry from the name of the file we are adding to our archive. In a while loop, we then read in our file using the FileInputStream and write it out to the

`ZipOutputStream`. After that is complete, we close the entry using the `closeEntry()` method of the `ZipOutputStream`, and then we close each of our open streams.

In this phrase, we have added just one file to our Zip archive, but the code would be easy to extend to add an arbitrary number of files to our Zip archive. The `ZipOutputStream` class supports both compressed and uncompressed entries.

9

Working with Directories and Files

A common task in most Java applications is working with the file system, which includes directories and files. In this chapter, we present phrases to help you work with files and directories in Java.

The main class we will use in this chapter is the `java.io.File` class. This class allows you to list, create, rename, and delete files, as well as work with directories.

Many of the phrases in this chapter have the possibility of throwing a `SecurityException`. In Java, the file system is protected by the Security Manager. For some applications, you might need to use a custom implementation of the Security Manager. Applets are the most restricted types of Java applications in terms of being able to access files and directories on the user's local machine. By taking advantage of the Security Manager and the related Security Policy Framework you can achieve fine-grained control over file and directory access. For more information about the security options available through Java, refer to the security documentation available on the official Java site:

http://java.sun.com/javase/technologies/security.jsp

For more information about the Security Manager, see the following tutorial available from Sun:

http://java.sun.com/docs/books/tutorial/essential/system/securityIntro.html

Creating a File

```
File f = new File("myfile.txt");
boolean result = f.createNewFile();
```

This phrase uses the `createNewFile()` method to create a new file with the filename specified when constructing the `File` object—in this case, `myfile.txt`. The `createNewFile()` method will return a `boolean` value of true if the file was successfully created and false if the specified filename already exists.

Another method is available in the `File` class for creating a temporary file: It's called `createTempFile()`. This is a static method on the `File` class. Here, we show how to use this method to create a temporary file:

```
File tmp =
   File.createTempFile("temp", "txt", "/temp");
```

The parameters that we pass to the `createTempFile()` method are the temp file's prefix, suffix, and the temp directory. Another version of this method is available that takes just two parameters and uses the default temp directory. For either form of the createTempFile() method to work, the specified file must not already exist.

If you are using temporary files, you'll also be interested in the deleteOnExit() method of the File class. You should call the deleteOnExit() method on a File object that represents a temporary file. Calling the deleteOnExit() method requests that the file be deleted automatically when the Java virtual machine terminates.

Renaming a File or Directory

```
File f = new File("myfile.txt");
File newFile = new File("newname.txt");
boolean result = f.renameTo(newFile);
```

In this phrase, we rename a file from myfile.txt to newname.txt. To accomplish this task, we have to create two File objects. The first File object is constructed with the current name of the file. Next, we create a new File object using the name we want to rename the file. We then call the renameTo() method on the original File object and pass in the File object that specifies the new filename. The renameTo() method will return a boolean value of true if the rename operation is successful and false if it fails for any reason.

This technique can also be used to rename a directory. The code for renaming a directory is exactly the same, except we pass the directory names to the File object constructors instead of file names. Here we show how this is done:

```
File f = new File("directoryA");
File newDirectory = new File("newDirectory");
boolean result = f.renameTo(newDirectory);
```

Remember that the new file or directory name must be specified in a `File` object that is passed to the `renameTo()` method. A common mistake is to attempt to pass a `String` containing the new file or directory name to the `renameTo()` method. Passing a `String` to the `renameTo()` method will generate a compile error.

Deleting a File or Directory

```
File f = new File("somefile.txt");
boolean result = f.delete();
```

Deleting a file using the `File` class is a simple task. We first create a `File` object specifying the name of the file that we want to delete. We then call the `File` object's `delete()` method. A `boolean` value of true is returned if the file was deleted successfully; otherwise, a false is returned.

The `delete()` method can also be used to delete a directory. To delete a directory, you would create the `File` object, specifying a directory name instead of a filename. Here, we show how you would delete a directory:

```
File directory = new File("files/images");
directory.delete();
```

The directory will only be deleted if it is empty. If the directory you are trying to delete using this method is not empty, the `delete()` method will return a `boolean` false value. If the file or directory that you are trying to delete does not exist, the `delete()` method will still return a false value, without throwing an exception.

Another useful method available related to deleting files and directories is the `deleteOnExit()` method of the File class. Calling the deleteOnExit() method requests that the file or directory represented by this File object be deleted automatically when the Java virtual machine terminates.

Changing File Attributes

```
File f = new File("somefile.txt");
boolean result = f.setReadOnly();
long time = (new Date()).getTime();
result = f.setLastModified(time);
```

The File object makes it easy to change the last modified time stamp on a file and the read/write status of a file. To perform these tasks, we use the setReadOnly() and setLastModified() methods of the File class. The setReadOnly() method, as you have probably guessed, sets the read/write status of the file on which the method is called to read-only. The setLastModified() method accepts a single parameter, specifying a time in milliseconds, and sets the file's last modified time to that time. The time value passed in is measured in milliseconds since the epoch (January 1, 1970, 00:00:00 GMT). Both of these methods will return a boolean value of true only if the operation is successful. If the operation fails for any reason, a value of false will be returned.

Getting the Size of a File

```
File file = new File("infilename");
long length = file.length();
```

In this phrase, we get the size of a file using the length() method on the File object. The length()

method will return the size of the file in bytes. If the file does not exist, a value of 0 is returned.

This method is often convenient to use prior to reading a file into a byte array. Using the `length()` method, you can determine the length of the file so that you know how large of a byte array you will need to hold the entire file contents. For example, the following code is often used for reading a file into a byte array:

```
File myFile = new File("myfile.bin");
InputStream is = new FileInputStream(myFile);
// Get the size of the file
long length = myFile.length();
if (length > Integer.MAX_VALUE) {
   // File is too large
}
byte[] bytes = new byte[(int)length];
int offset = 0;
int numRead = 0;
while (offset < bytes.length
   && (numRead=is.read(bytes, offset, bytes.length-
offset)) >= 0) {
   offset += numRead;
}
is.close();
```

Determining if a File or Directory Exists

```
boolean exists = (new File("filename")).exists();
if (exists) {
   // File or directory exists
}
else {
   // File or directory does not exist
}
```

In this phrase, we use the `exists()` method on the `File` object to determine if the file or directory represented by the `File` object exists. The `exists()` method will return true if the file or directory exists, otherwise it will return false.

Moving a File or Directory

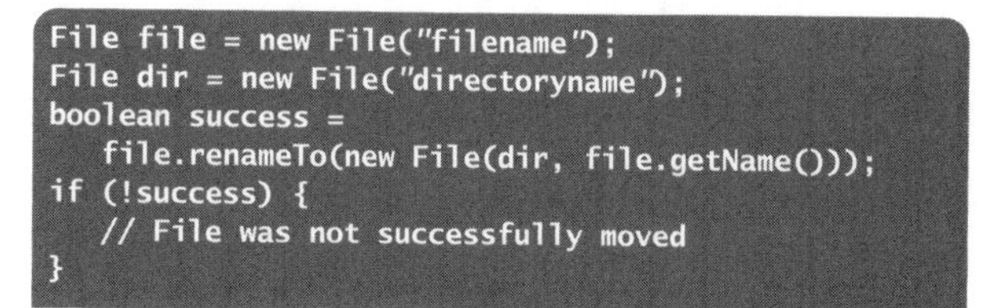

```
File file = new File("filename");
File dir = new File("directoryname");
boolean success =
   file.renameTo(new File(dir, file.getName()));
if (!success) {
   // File was not successfully moved
}
```

The `renameTo()` method of the `File` class allows us to move a file or directory into a different directory. In this phrase, we create a `File` object to represent the file or directory we are moving. We create another `File` object representing the destination directory that we are moving the file or directory into. We then call the `renameTo()` method on the file being moved and pass it a single `File` object parameter. The `File` object passed as a parameter is constructed using the destination directory and the original file name. If the move operation is successful, the `renameTo()` method will return a boolean true value. If the move fails, a boolean false is returned.

When you use the `renameTo()` method, keep in mind that many aspects of its behavior are platform dependent. Some of these platform dependent behaviours are noted in the JavaDoc for this method. They include the following:

- The rename operation might not be able to move a file from one filesystem to another.
- The rename operation might not be atomic. This means that the implementation of the rename operation may consist of multiple steps at the operating system level. This could lead to problems in severe conditions such as power failure between steps.
- The rename operation might not succeed if a file with the destination abstract pathname already exists.

When using this method, you should always check the return value to make sure that the rename operation was successful.

Getting an Absolute Filename Path from a Relative Filename Path

```
File file = new File("somefile.txt");
File absPath = file.getAbsoluteFile();
```

In this phrase, we get an absolute path for a file for which we specify a relative path. An absolute pathname gives the full path for a file starting from the file system's root directory, i.e. `c:\project\book\somefile.txt`. A relative pathname specifies a file's name and path relative to the current directory, i.e. `somefile.txt` if the current directory is `c:\project\book`. In many cases, a relative pathname consists of only the filename. The `getAbsoluteFile()` method of the `File` class returns a `File` object representing the absolute filename for the file represented by the `File` object on which it is called.

There is a similar method called `getAbsolutePath()` that returns the absolute path as a `String` instead of as a `File` object. The code below shows this method:

```
File file = new File("filename.txt");
String absPath = file.getAbsolutePath();
```

In this example, `absPath` would contain the string "`c:\project\book\somefile.txt`".

Determining if a Filename Path is a File or Directory

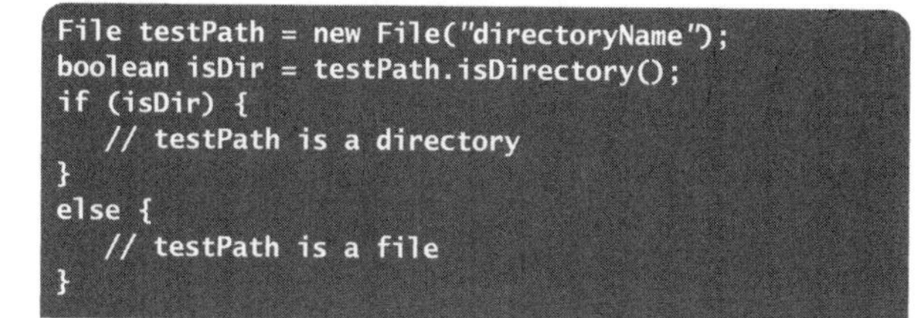

```
File testPath = new File("directoryName");
boolean isDir = testPath.isDirectory();
if (isDir) {
   // testPath is a directory
}
else {
   // testPath is a file
}
```

In this phrase, we determine if a given `File` object represents a file or a directory. The `isDirectory()` method of the `File` class will return true if the `File` object on which it is called represents a directory, and it will return false if the `File` object represents a file.

This method is useful when you want to write a method that will traverse all of the files and directories under a given directory. Perhaps you want to write a method that will list all of the files under a specified directory and you want the method to recurse into all the subdirectories contained within the specified directory. As you step through each listing contained in a directory, you would use the isDirectory() method to determine if the listing represents a file or a directory. Below is an example of such a method that makes use of the isDirectory() method:

```
static void listAllFiles(File dir) {
   String[] files = dir.list();
   for (int i = 0; i < files.length; i++) {
      File f = new File(dir, files[i]);
      if (f.isDirectory()) {
         listAllFiles(f);
      }
      else {
         System.out.println(f.getAbsolutePath());
      }
   }
}
```

If you call this method and pass in a File object representing a directory, it will print the full-path names of all files contained within that directory and all of its subdirectories.

There is also an isFile() method on the File class that will return true if the File object on which it is called represents a file, otherwise it will return false.

Listing a Directory

```
File directory = new File("users/tim");
String[] result = directory.list();
```

We can also use the File class to list the contents of a directory. In this phrase, we use the list() method of the File class to get a String array containing all the files and subdirectories contained within the directory specified by the File object. If the directory does not exist, a null value is returned. The strings returned are filenames and simple directory names; they are not complete paths. Also, the results are not guaranteed to be in any defined order.

An alternate implementation of the `list()` method is also available. It accepts a `java.io.FilenameFilter` parameter and allows you to filter the files and directories returned in the list results. Use of this method is shown here:

```
File directory = new File("users/tim");
FilenameFilter fileFilter = new HTMLFileFilter();
String[] result = directory.list(fileFilter);
```

The corresponding implementation of the `HTMLFileFilter` class used above is shown here:

```
class HTMLFileFilter extends FilenameFilter {
   public boolean accept(File f) {
      return f.isDirectory() || f.getName()
      .toLowerCase() .endsWith(".html"));
   }
   public String getDescription() }
      return "/html files";
}
```

`FilenameFilter` is an interface with one defined method, `accept()`. The `accept()` method takes two parameters—a `File` object and a `String` object. The `File` object specifies the directory in which the file was found, and the `String` object specifies the name of the file. The `accept()` method returns true if the file should be included in the list; otherwise, it returns false. In this example, we have created a filter that will cause the `list()` method to include only files that end with the .html extention.

If the filter passed in is null, this method behaves identical to the previous `list()` method with no parameters.

In addition to the `list()` methods, the `File` class also has two versions of a `listFiles()` method. The `listFiles()` method returns an array of `File` objects instead of a string array. The no parameter form of this method is shown here:

```
File directory = new File("users/tim");
File[] result = directory.listFiles();
```

The resulting `File` objects contain relative or absolute pathnames, depending on the `File` object from which the `listFiles()` method was called. In the previous example, if the `directory File` object contained an absolute path, the results would contain absolute pathnames. If the `directory File` object contained a relative pathname, the results would have relative pathnames.

There is also a version of `listFiles()` that accepts a `FileFilter` parameter, similar to the example we showed for the `list()` method. We show an example of this here:

```
File directory = new File("users/tim");
FileFilter fileFilter = new HTMLFileFilter();
String[] result = directory.listFiles(fileFilter);
```

The corresponding implementation of the `HTMLFileFilter` class used above is shown here:

```
class HTMLFileFilter extends FileFilter {
   public boolean accept(File f) {
      return f.isDirectory() ||
f.getName().toLowerCase().endsWith(".html");
   }
   public String getDescription() {
```

```
        return ".html files";
    }
}
```

FileFilter is an interface with two defined methods, accept() and getDescription(). Unlike the accept() method of FilenameFilter, the accept() method of FileFilter takes only one parameter, a File object. The File object specifies either a file or directory. The accept() method returns true if the file or directory should be included in the list; otherwise, it returns false. In this example, we have created a filter that will cause the list() method to include only files that end with the .html extention and directories.

Creating a New Directory

```
boolean success = (new File("users/tim")).mkdir();
```

In this phrase, we use the mkdir() method of the File class to create a new directory. This method will return true if the directory is successfully created. If the directory cannot be created, the method returns false. The mkdir() method will only create a directory if all specified parent directories already exist. In the preceding phrase, the users directory must already exist for this execution of mkdir() to successfully create the users/tim directory.

A similar method will allow you to create an entire directory tree, including all parent directories, if they do not exist. This is the mkdirs() method on the File class. Here, we show an example using this method:

```
boolean success =
   (new File("/users/tim/web")).mkdirs( );
```

In the preceding example, the `mkdirs()` method will create any of the directories (`users`, `tim`, `web`) that do not exist.

10

Network Clients

Most applications written today require some network features. The standalone Java application is a relatively rare occurrence. Therefore, this chapter on network clients is valuable to most developers writing Java applications today.

Network program involves communication between a client and a server. The client is typically the application making some request for content or services, and the server is a network-based application that serves content and services to many clients. In this chapter, we focus on the client. In Chapter 11, "Network Servers," we'll provide server-related phrases.

Except for a phrase that deals with reading a web page via HTTP, the phrases in this chapter are all at the level of socket-based programming. Sockets are a low-level networking implementation. For most of your needs, you will want to use a protocol that is at a layer above sockets, such as HTTP, SMTP, or POP. Additional Java or third-party APIs are available for dealing with these higher level network protocols.

The `java.net` package provides the functionality for client-side networking that we will use in this chapter.

J2EE, which is not covered in this book, offers many more network-based services including full support for server-side Java web development. Network-related technologies included in J2EE include servlets, EJB, and JMS.

Contacting a Server

```
String serverName = "www.timothyfisher.com";
Socket sock = new Socket(serverName, 80);
```

In this phrase, we connect to a server via TCP/IP using Java's `Socket` class. During construction of the `sock` instance in our phrase, a socket connection will be made to the server specified by `serverName`—in this case, `www.timothyfisher.com` and port 80.

Whenever a `Socket` is created, you must be sure to close the socket when you are finished with it by calling the `close()` method on the `Socket` instance you are working with.

Java supports other ways of connecting to a server that we won't discuss details of here. For example, you could use the `URL` class to open a URL and read from it. See the phrase "Reading a Web Page via HTTP" in this chapter for more details on using the `URL` class.

Finding IP Addresses and Domain Names

```
// find IP address for given domain
String hostName = www.timothyfisher.com";
```

```
String ip =
   InetAddress.getByName(hostName).getHostAddress();

// find domain name for ip address
String ipAddress = "66.43.127.5";
String hostName =
   InetAddres.getByName(ipAddress).getHostName();
```

In this phrase, we get a hostname when you know the IP address of a remote host, and we get an IP address when you start with the hostname of the remote host. To accomplish both of these tasks, we rely on the `InetAddress` class.

We use the `getByName()` static method of the `InetAddress` class to create an `InetAddress` instance. We can pass either an IP address or a hostname into the `getByName()` method to create the `InetAddress` instance. Once we have the `InetAddress` instance, we can call the `getHostAddress()` method to return the IP address as a `String`. If we already know the IP address, we can call the `getHostName()` method to return the hostname as a `String`. If the host name cannot be resolved, the `getHostName()` method will return the IP address.

Handling Network Errors

```
try {
 // connect to network host
 // perform network IO
}
catch (UnknownHostException ex) {
    System.err.println("Unknown host.");
}
catch (NoRouteToHostException ex) {
    System.err.println("Unreachable host.");

}
```

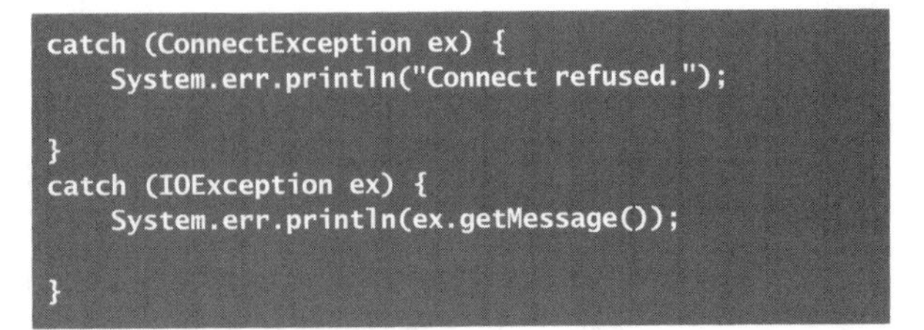

```
catch (ConnectException ex) {
    System.err.println("Connect refused.");

}
catch (IOException ex) {
    System.err.println(ex.getMessage());

}
```

In this phrase, we illustrate the series of exceptions you should attempt to catch when performing network operations.

The first exception we try to catch is the `UnknownHostException`. This is a subclass of `IOException` and is thrown to indicate that the IP address of a host could not be determined.

`NoRouteToHostException` and the `ConnectException` are subclasses of `SocketException`. `NoRouteToHostException` signals that an error occurred while attempting to connect a socket to a remote address and port. Typically, the remote host cannot be reached because of a problem with an intervening firewall or router. `ConnectException` is thrown if a connection is refused to the remote host. `IOException` is a more general purpose exception that can also be thrown from networking calls.

The phrases throughout this chapter and Chapter 11, "Network Servers," do not include error handling. Catching these exceptions is what you would do in your Java applications that use networking functionality.

Reading Text

```
BufferedReader in =
   new BufferedReader(new InputStreamReader(
      socket.getInputStream()));
String text = in.readLine();
```

This phrase assumes that we've previously created a socket to the server from which we want to read text. See the phrase "Contacting a Server" in this chapter for more details on creating the socket instance. Given the socket instance, we call the `getInputStream()` method to get a reference to the socket's input stream. With that, we create an `InputStreamReader` and use it to instantiate a `BufferedReader` for reading in the text across the network. The `readLine()` method of the `BufferedReader`.

Using the `BufferedReader` as we do in this phrase allows for efficient reading of characters, arrays, and lines. If we were interested in reading only a very small amount of data, we could do this directly from the `InputStreamReader`, without using a `BufferedReader`. Here, we show how you could read data into a character array using only an `InputStreamReader`:

```
InputStreamReader in =
   new InputStreamReader(socket.getInputStream()));
String text = in.read(charArray, offset, length);
```

In this example, data would be read from the input stream into the array of characters specified by `charArray`. The characters would be placed in the array starting at an offset specified by the `offset` parameter, and the maximum number of characters read is specified by the `length` parameter.

Writing Text

```
PrintWriter out =
   new PrintWriter(socket.getOutputStream(), true);
out.print(msg);
out.flush();
```

This phrase assumes that we've previously created a socket to the server from which we want to write text. See the phrase "Contacting a Server" in this chapter for more details on creating the socket instance. Given the socket instance, we call the `getOutputStream()` method to get a reference to the socket's output stream. With that, we instantiate a `PrintWriter` for writing text across the network to the server with which we are connected. The second parameter that we pass to the `PrintWriter` constructor in this phrase sets the auto-flush option. Setting this to true will cause the `println()`, `printf()`, and `format()` methods to automatically flush the output buffer. In our phrase, we use the `print()` method; thus, we must follow that by a call to the `flush()` method to force the data across the network.

Reading Binary Data

```
DataInputStream in =
   new DataInputStream(socket.getInputStream());
in.readUnsignedByte();
```

In this phrase, we show how to read binary data across a network. This phrase assumes that we've previously created a socket to the server from which we want to read text. See the phrase "Contacting a Server" in this chapter for more details on creating the socket instance.

In this phrase, we call the `getInputStream()` method of the socket instance to obtain a reference to the socket's input stream. Passing the input stream as a parameter, we instantiate a `DataInputStream`, which we can use to read binary data across the network. We use the `readUnsignedByte()` method to read a single unsigned byte across the network.

If the volume of data that you are reading is large, it will be more efficient to wrap the socket's input stream in a `BufferedInputStream` instance. Here, we show how this is done:

```
DataInputStream in = new DataInputStream(
   new BufferedInputStream(
      socket.getInputStream()));
```

Here, instead of directly passing the socket's input stream to the `DataInputStream` constructor, we first create a `BufferedInputStream` instance and pass that to the `DataInputStream` constructor.

In this phrase, we used the `readUnsignedByte()` method, but `DataInputStream` has many other methods available to read data into any primitive Java data type. The available methods for reading binary data include: `read()`, `readBoolean()`, `readByte()`, `readChar()`, `readDouble()`, `readFloat()`, `readInt()`, `readLong()`, `readShort()`, `readUnsignedByte()`, and `readUnsignedShort()`. See the JavaDoc for details on using these methods and other methods of the `DataInputStream` class: http://java.sun.com/j2se/1.5.0/docs/api/java/io/DataInputStream.html

Writing Binary Data

```
DataOutputStream out =
   new DataOutputStream(socket.getOutputStream());
out.write(byteArray, 0, 10);
```

In a previous phrase in this chapter, "Writing Text," we showed how to write text data across a network. In this phrase, we show how to write binary data across a network. This phrase assumes that we've previously created a socket to the server from which we want to write text. See the phrase "Contacting a Server" in this chapter for more details on creating the socket instance.

In this phrase, we call the `getOutputStream()` method of the socket instance to obtain a reference to the socket's output stream. We then instantiate a `DataOutputStream`, which we can use to write binary data across the network. We use the `write()` method to write an array of bytes across the network. The `write()` method takes three parameters. The first parameter is a `byte[]` to get the bytes to write from. The second parameter is an offset into the byte array to begin writing from. The third parameter is the number of bytes that you want to write. So, in this phrase, we write bytes from the `byteArray` array, beginning at offset 0, and we write a total of 10 bytes.

If the volume of data that you are writing is large, it will be more efficient to wrap the socket's output stream in a `BufferedOutputStream` instance. Here, we show how this is done:

```
DataOutputStream out = new DataOutputStream(
   new BufferedOutputStream(
      socket.getOutputStream()));
```

Here, instead of directly passing the socket's output stream to the DataOutputStream constructor, we first create a BufferedOutputStream instance and pass that to the DataOutputStream constructor.

In this phrase, we used the write() method, but the DataOutputStream has many other methods available to write data from any primitive Java data type. The available methods for writing binary data include: write(), writeBoolean(), writeByte(), writeBytes(), writeChar(), writeChars(), writeDouble(), writeFloat(), writeInt(), writeLong(), and writeShort(). See the JavaDoc for details on using these methods and other methods of the DataOutputStream class: http://java.sun.com/j2se/1.5.0/docs/api/java/io/DataOutputStream.html

Reading Serialized Data

```
ObjectInputStream in =
   new ObjectInputStream(socket.getInputStream());
Object o = in.readObject();
```

Java enables object instances to be serialized and written either to a file or across a network. In this phrase, we show how you can read from a network socket an object that has been serialized. This phrase assumes that we've previously created a socket to the server with which we want to communicate. See the phrase "Contacting a Server" in this chapter for more details on creating the socket instance.

In this phrase, we call the getInputStream() method of the socket instance to get a reference to the socket's input stream. Using this, we can instantiate an ObjectInputStream instance. The ObjectInputStream class is used to deserialize primitive data and objects previously written using an `ObjectOutputStream`. We use the `readObject()` method of the `ObjectInputStream` to read an object from the stream. We could then cast the object to its expected type. For example, if we were reading a `Date` object from the stream, we would use the following line to read it:

```
Date aDate = (Date)in.readObject();
```

All data fields that are non-transient and non-static will be restored to the value they had when the object was serialized.

Only objects that support the `java.io.Serializable` or `java.io.Externalizable` interface can be read from streams. When implementing a serializable class it is strongly recommended that you declare a `serialVersionUID` data member. This field provides a version number that is used during deserialization to verify that the sender and receiver of a serialized object have loaded classes for that object that are compatible with respect to serialization. If you do not explicitly declare this field, a default `serialVersionUID` will be calculated for you. The default `serialVersionUID` is highly sensitive to all class details. You may make minor changes in a class and wish to keep the same version number as you consider it to still be compatible with the current version, therefore it is beneficial to declare your own `serialVersionUID`.

Writing Serialized Data

```
ObjectOutputStream out =
   new ObjectOutputStream(socket.getOutputStream());
out.writeObject(myObject);
```

Java enables object instances to be serialized and written either to a file or across a network. In this phrase, we show how you can write a serialized object to a network socket. This phrase assumes that we've previously created a socket to the server with which we want to communicate. See the phrase "Contacting a Server" in this chapter for more details on creating the socket instance.

In this phrase, we call the `getOutputStream()` method of the socket instance to get a reference to the socket's output stream. Using this, we can instantiate an `ObjectOutputStream` instance. The `ObjectOutputStream` class is used to serialize primitive data and objects. We use the `writeObject()` method of the `ObjectOutputStream` to write an object to the stream.

All data fields that are non-transient and non-static will be preserved in the serialization and restored when the object is deserialized. Only objects that support the `java.io.Serializable` interface can be written to streams.

Reading a Web Page via HTTP

```
URL url = new URL("http://www.timothyfisher.com");
HttpURLConnection http = new HttpURLConnection(url);
InputStream in = http.getInputStream();
```

In this phrase, we go beyond socket level network programming and show you an additional way of reading data from a network. Java supports communication with a URL over HTTP with the `HttpURLConnection` class. We instantiate a `URL` instance by passing a valid URL string to the `URL` constructor. We then instantiate an `HttpURLConnection` by passing the `url` instance into the HttpURLConnection constructor. The getInputStream() method is called to get an input stream for reading data from the URL connection. Using the input stream, we could then read the contents of the web page.

You can also read the contents of a URL using the URL class directly. Here is an example of how we do this using only the URL class:

```
URL url = new URL("http://www.timothyfisher.com");
url.getContent();
```

The getContent() method returns an Object. The object returned can be an InputStream or an object containing the data. A common example would be for the getContent() method to return a String object containing the contents of a URL. The getContent() method that we used here is actually shorthand for the following code:

```
url.openConnection.getContent();
```

The openConnection() method of the URL class returns an URLConnection object. This is the object that the getContent() method is actually implemented in.

The HttpURLConnection provides HTTP specific methods not available in the more general URL or URLConnection classes. For example, we can use the getResponseCode() method to get the status code from an HTTP response message. HTTP also defines a protocol for redirecting a request to a different server. The HttpURLConnection class has methods that understand this feature as well. For example, if you want to make a request to a server and follow any redirects that the server returns, you can use the following code to set this option:

```
URL url = new URL("http://www.timothyfisher.com");
HttpURLConnection http = new HttpURLConnection(url);
http.setFollowRedircts(true);
```

This option is actually set to be true by default, so a more useful scenario might be setting the follow redirects option to false if, for some reason, you do not want to be automatically redirected to a server other than the one that you initially made the request on. For example, you might want to consider this for certain security applications from which you only trust specified servers.

Web pages that contain sensitive data are usually protected by a security protocol called Secure Sockets Layer, commonly referred to as SSL. An SSL protected page is referred to using `https` in the URL string, as opposed to `http`. The standard Java JDK does include an implementation of SSL as part of the Java Secure Socket Extension (JSSE). In order to retrieve an SSL protected page, you would use the `HttpsURLConnection` class instead of the `HttpURLConnection` class. The HttpsURLConnection class transparently handles all of the details of the SSL protocol for you. For more details on using SSL and other security features provided by JSSE, see the JSSE reference guide provided by Sun at: http://java.sun.com/j2se/1.5.0/docs/guide/security/jsse/JSSERefGuide.html.

11

Network Servers

In the real world, you are probably much more likely to be writing network client code than network server code. Many applications integrate both client and server features, and fortunately Java provides excellent support for both.

The `java.net` package provides the functionality for server-side networking that we will use in this chapter.

J2EE, which is not covered in this book, offers many more network-based services, including full support for server-side Java web development. Network-related technologies included in J2EE include servlets, EJB, and JMS.

Creating a Server and Accepting a Request

```
public static final short PORT = 9988;
ServerSocket server = new ServerSocket(PORT);
while ((clientSock = server.accept( )) != null) {
    // Process client request
}
```

In this phrase, we use a ServerSocket instance to create a server listening on port 9988. We pass the port that we want the server to listen on to the constructor of the ServerSocket. Once the server socket is created, we call the accept() method to wait for a client connection. The accept() method blocks until a connection with a client is made. When a client connection is made, a new Socket instance is returned.

If a security manager is being used, the security manager's checkAccept() method is called with clientSock.getInetAddress().getHostAddress() and clientSock.getPort() as its arguments to ensure the operation is allowed. This could result in a SecurityException.

The phrases in this chapter all make use of the ServerSocket class. The ServerSocket class is used by a server to wait for and make connections with a client. As seen in this phrase, when you first create a ServerSocket class, you specify a port to listen on for incoming requests. The ServerSocket class itself is not used for communication with a client, but only to establish a connection with the client. When ServerSocket accepts a client connection, a regular Socket instance is returned. The Socket instance is what you use to communicate with the client.

See the related phrase, "Handling Multiple Clients" for information on how you should write your code when you expect to handle many simultaneous client requests.

Returning a Response

```
Socket clientSock = serverSocket.accept();
DataOutputStream out =
  new DataOutputStream(
        clientSock.getOutputStream());
out.writeInt(someValue);
out.close();
```

This phrase shows an example of how to return a response from a server to a client. The `accept()` method of the `ServerSocket` instance will return a `Socket` instance when a connection is made with a client. We then get the socket's output stream by calling the `getOutputStream()` method of the socket. We use the output stream to instantiate a `DataOutputStream`, which we then call the `writeInt()` method on to write an integer value, sending binary data to the client. Finally, we close the socket using the `close()` method of the `Socket`.

In this phrase, we use the `write()` method, but the `DataOutputStream` has many other methods available to write data from any primitive Java data type. The available methods for writing binary data include: `write()`, `writeBoolean()`, `writeByte()`, `writeBytes()`, `writeChar()`, `writeChars()`, `writeDouble()`, `writeFloat()`, `writeInt()`, `writeLong()`, and `writeShort()`. See the JavaDoc for details on using these methods and other methods of the `DataOutputStream` class:http://java.sun.com/j2se/1.5.0/docs/api/java/io/DataOutputStream.html

If we wanted to write text data to the client, we could use the following code:

```
Socket clientSock = serverSocket.accept();
PrintWriter out =
   new PrintWriter(new OutputStreamWriter(
          clientSock.getOutputStream()), true);
out.println("Hello World");
out.close();
```

Instead of creating a `DataOutputStream`, here we create an `OutputStreamWriter` and a `PrintWriter`. We use the `print()` method of the `PrintWriter` to write a text string to the client. The second parameter that we pass to the `PrintWriter` constructor sets the auto-flush option. Setting this to true will cause the `println()`, `printf()`, and `format()` methods to automatically flush the output buffer. In our phrase, we use the `println()` method; thus, it is not necessary to explicitly call the `flush()` method. As always, when we are done using the `PrintWriter`, we call the `close()` method to close the stream.

Returning an Object

```
Socket clientSock = serverSocket.accept();
ObjectOutputStream os = new ObjectOutputStream(
    clientSock.getOutputStream( ));

// return an object
os.writeObject(new Date());
os.close();
```

In this phrase, we return a serialized object to a client. We get a `Socket` instance returned from the `accept()`

method of the `ServerSocket` after making a connection with a client. We then create an `ObjectOutputStream` instance, passing the output stream obtained from the client socket. An `ObjectOutputStream` is used to write primitive datatypes and graphs of Java objects to an `OutputStream`. In this example, we write a `Date` object to the output stream and then close the stream.

The `writeObject()` method causes the object passed as a parameter to be serialized. In this phrase, this is a `Date` object. All data fields that are non-transient and non-static will be preserved in the serialization and restored when the object is deserialized. Only objects that support the `java.io.Serializable` interface can be serialized.

An interesting alternative to the `ObjectOutputStream` and `ObjectInputStream` classes is an open source project from codehaus.org called XStream. XStream provides alternative implementations of `ObjectInputStream` and `ObjectOutputStream`, enabling streams of objects to be serialized or deserialized from XML. The standard `ObjectInputStream` class uses a binary format for the serialized data. The serialized output of the XStream classes provides the serialized classes in easy-to-read XML format. You can find more information about XStream and download it from: http://xstream.codehaus.org/index.html

Handling Multiple Clients

```
while (true) {
    Socket clientSock = socket.accept();
    new Handler(clientSock).start();
}
```

To handle multiple clients, we create a thread for each incoming request that we are processing.

In this phrase, we create a new thread to handle the incoming client connection immediately after accepting the connection. This frees our server listener thread to continue listening for other client connections. In the phrase, we are in an infinite `while` loop so that after a thread is spawned to handle an incoming request, the server immediately goes back to waiting for another request. The `Handler` class that we use to start the thread from must be a subclass of the `Thread` class, or it must implement the `Runnable` interface. The code used in the phrase would be correct if the `Handler` class is a subclass of the `Thread` class. If the `Handler` class instead implements the `Runnable` interface, the thread start code would change to the following:

```
Thread thd = new Thread(new Handler(clientSock));
thd.start();
```

An example of a simple `Handler` class extending the `Thread` class is shown here:

```
class Handler extends Thread {
   Socket sock;

   Handler(Socket socket) {
      this.sock = socket;
   }

   public void run() {
      DataInputStream in =
         new DataInputStream(sock.getInputStream());
      PrintStream out =
```

```
            new PrintStream(sock.getOutputStream(),
                  true);

        // handle client request

        sock.close();
    }
}
```

This class could be used to handle incoming client requests. We don't show the details of handling a specific request in the code. When the `start()` method of this class is called, as in our phrase, the `run()` method that we have defined is executed. The `start()` method is implemented in the `Thread` base class, and we do not have to override that in our `Handler` implementation.

When creating a multi-threaded solution such as we've outlined in this phrase, you might also want to consider using thread pooling. With a thread pool, rather than creating a new thread for each incoming request, a pool of threads is created at application start time. The thread pool has a fixed number of threads that execute tasks. Using a thread pool will prevent the application from creating an excessive number of threads which could impede performance. A very good article describing thread pooling is available from http://www.informit.com/articles/article.asp?p=30483&seqNum=3&rl=1

For more information about using threads, see Chapter 15, "Using Threads."

Serving HTTP Content

```
Socket client = serverSocket.accept();
BufferedReader in =
   new BufferedReader(new InputStreamReader(
                        client.getInputStream()));
// before serving a response, typically you would
// read the client input and process the request.
PrintWriter out =
   new PrintWriter(client.getOutputStream());
out.println("HTTP/1.1 200");
out.println("Content-Type: text/html");
String html = "<html><head><title>Test Response" +
   "</title></head><body>Just a test</body></html>";
out.println("Content-length: " + html.length());
out.println(html);
out.flush();
out.close();
```

In this phrase, we show an example of serving a very simple piece of HTML content via HTTP. We accept a connection with a client, create a `BufferedReader` to read the client's request, and create a `PrintWriter`, which we use to send HTML via HTTP back to the client. The data that we write to the `PrintWriter` is the minimum necessary to create a valid HTTP response message. Our response consists of three HTTP header fields and our HTML data. We start our response by specifying the HTTP version and a response code in this line:

```
out.println("HTTP/1.1 200");
```

We are returning HTTP version 1.1 and a response code of `200`. The response code of `200` indicates a successful request. In the next line, we specify the content type we are returning as HTML. We could return content types other than HTML and still have a valid HTTP response message. For example, the following would specify that our response is plaintext instead of HTML:

```
out.println("Content-Type: text/plain");
```

The next thing we write is the Content-length header. This specifies the length of the actual content being returned and does not include the header fields. After that, we write the actual HTML message that we are returning. Finally, we flush and close the `BufferedReader` stream using the `flush()` and `close()` methods.

NOTE: Although this technique is useful for simple HTTP serving requirements, I would not recommend trying to write your own complete HTTP server from scratch in Java. An excellent HTTP server is available freely as open source that is part of the Apache Jakarta project. This is the Tomcat server. You can get more information about Tomcat and download it from http://jakarta.apache.org/tomcat/. Not only does Tomcat serve HTTP, but it also contains a servlet container to handle Java Servlets and JSPs.

12

Sending and Receiving Email

Email has been called the killer application of the Internet and is used in many applications. It is very likely that at some point you will want to support email in one of your own Java applications. Fortunately, Java has excellent support for integrating email into your Java applications using the JavaMail API. The JavaMail API is an extension to the core Java. Because of this, you have to download it separately. It is not a part of the standard JDK download. The relevant classes that make up the JavaMail API are in the `javax.mail` package. The current JavaMail API requires JDK 1.4 or newer. Earlier versions of the JDK require an older version of the JavaMail API.

This chapter covers the topics of sending and receiving email from a Java application. Integrating email capability into your Java application is a great addition to many applications. Some real world examples of where this might be useful included sending email alerts from an application, automatic emailing of logs and reports, and user communication.

Overview of JavaMail API

JavaMail provides functionality for sending and receiving email. Service providers plug in to the JavaMail API providing implementations of various email protocols. The Sun implementation includes service providers for IMAP, POP3 and SMTP. JavaMail is also a part of enterprise Java in J2EE.

You can download the Java Mail extension from: http://java.sun.com/products/javamail/downloads/index.html

To use the JavaMail API, you must also download and install the JavaBeans Activation Framework extension (JAF). JAF can be downloaded from: http://java.sun.com/products/javabeans/jaf/downloads/index.html

In addition to the phrases covered in this chapter, you can find complete details on using the JavaMail API at the JavaMail link on the Sun Developer Network: http://java.sun.com/products/javamail/index.jsp

Sending Email

```
Properties props = new Properties( );
props.put("mail.smtp.host", "mail.yourhost.com");
Session session =
   Session.getDefaultInstance(props, null);

Message msg = new MimeMessage(session);
msg.setFrom(new
   InternetAddress("tim@timothyfisher.com"));
InternetAddress toAddress =
   new InternetAddress("kerry@timothyfisher.com");
```

```
msg.addRecipient(Message.RecipientType.TO,
                  toAddress);
msg.setSubject("Test Message");
msg.setText("This is the body of my message.");
Transport.send(msg);
```

In this phrase, we send a plaintext email message using an SMTP server. There are six basic steps that you should always follow when you want to send email using the JavaMail API. These steps are identified here:

1. Create a `java.util.Properties` object, which you will use to pass information about the mail server.
2. Put the hostname of the SMTP mail server into the `Properties` object. Also, put any other properties you want to set into the `Properties` object.
3. Create `Session` and `Message` objects.
4. Set recipients' and sender's email addresses and the message subject in the `Message` object.
5. Set the message text in the `Message` object.
6. Call the `Transport.send()` method to send the message.

We follow each of these steps in this phrase to create and send an email message. Note that the From and To addresses are created as `InternetAddress` objects. An `InternetAddress` object represents a valid email address. An exception will be thrown if you attempt to create an `InternetAddress` object using an invalid email address format. When you specify the To recipients, you also specify the type of the recipient. Valid types are TO, CC, and BCC. These are represented by the following constants:

```
Message.RecipientType.TO
Message.RecipientType.CC
Message.RecipientType.BCC
```

The `Message` class is an abstract class defined in the `javax.mail` package. There is one subclass that implements the `Message` class that is part of the standard JavaMail reference implementation. This is the `MimeMessage` class, which is the implementation we use in our phrase here. This implementation represents a MIME style email message. You should be able to use this for most, if not all, of your email needs.

In this phrase, we use the `Properties` object to pass only the SMTP mail host. This is the only required property that you must set. There are additional properties that you can set, though.

NOTE: See the `javax.mail` package overview in the JavaDoc for additional detail on other email related properties that you can pass in the `Properties` object:
http://java.sun.com/javaee/5/docs/api/javax/mail/package-summary.html

Sending MIME Email

```
String html =
    "<html><head><title>Java Mail</title></head>" +
    "<body>Some HTML content.</body></html>";

Multipart mp = new MimeMultipart();
BodyPart textPart = new MimeBodyPart( );
textPart.setText("This is the message body.");
BodyPart htmlPart = new MimeBodyPart( );
htmlPart.setContent(html, "text/html");
mp.addBodyPart(textPart);
mp.addBodyPart(htmlPart);
msg.setContent(mp);
Transport.send(msg);
```

MIME stands for Multimedia Internet Mail Extensions. MIME is supported by all major email clients and is the standard way of including attachments to messages. MIME allows you to attach a variety of media types, such as images, video, and `.pdf` files to an email message. The JavaMail API also supports MIME messages, and it is nearly as easy to create a message with attachments as a MIME message as it is to create a standard plaintext message.

In this phrase, we create and send a MIME message containing a plaintext body and an HTML attachment. To create a multipart message, we use the `MultiPart` class, which is a part of the `javax.mail` package. The `MimeMultiPart` class, in the `javax.mail.internet` package, provides a concrete implementation of the MultiPart abstract class and uses MIME conventions for the multipart data. The `MimeMultiPart` class allows us to add multiple body parts, represented as `MimeBodyPart` objects. We set a body part's content using the `setText()` method for plaintext body parts or the `setContent()` method for other types of body parts. When we use the `setContent()` method, we pass an object that holds the body part, along with a string specifying the MIME type we are adding. In our phrase, we add an HTML body part, so we specify the MIME type as `text/html`.

The code in shown in the phrase focusing on the MIME specific parts of sending a MIME message. The example below is a more complete example of sending a MIME email message including all steps necessary to accomplish the task:

```
Properties props = new Properties( );
props.put("mail.smtp.host", "mail.yourhost.com");
```

```
Session session =
   Session.getDefaultInstance(props, null);

Message msg = new MimeMessage(session);
msg.setFrom(new
   InternetAddress("tim@timothyfisher.com"));
InternetAddress toAddress =
   new InternetAddress("kerry@timothyfisher.com");
msg.addRecipient(Message.RecipientType.TO,
                  toAddress);
msg.setSubject("Test Message");
String html =
    "<html><head><title>Java Mail</title></head>" +
    "<body>Some HTML content.</body></html>";
Multipart mp = new MimeMultipart();
BodyPart textPart = new MimeBodyPart( );
textPart.setText("This is the message body.");
BodyPart htmlPart = new MimeBodyPart( );
htmlPart.setContent(html, "text/html");
mp.addBodyPart(textPart);
mp.addBodyPart(htmlPart);
msg.setContent(mp);
Transport.send(msg);
```

NOTE: The Internet Assigned Numbers Authority (IANA) provides a good reference of all the standard MIME media types on their website. The site also provides an application for registering a new MIME type. If you don't feel that any existing MIME types are suitable for your content, you can use this application to request a new standard MIME media type be created that supports your content type. The IANA website is at: http://www.iana.org

The MIME media types can be found on the IANA site at: http://www.iana.org/assignments/media-types/

Reading Email

```
Properties props = new Properties();
Session session =
   Session.getDefaultInstance(props, null);
Store store = session.getStore("pop3");
store.connect(host, username, password);

Folder folder = store.getFolder("INBOX");
folder.open(Folder.READ_ONLY);

Message message[] = folder.getMessages();
for (int i=0, n=message.length; i<n; i++) {
   System.out.println(i + ": " +
      message[i].getFrom()[0] + "\t" +
      message[i].getSubject());
   String content =
      message[i].getContent().toString();
   System.out.print(content.substring(0,100));
}

folder.close(false);
store.close();
```

In this phrase, we connect to a POP3 email server and retrieve all messages in the INBOX folder. The JavaMail API makes this task quite easy to perform. Here are the general steps you perform when using the JavaMail API to read messages from a POP mail server:

1. Get a `Session` object.
2. Get a `Store` object from the `Session` object.
3. Create a `Folder` object for the folder that you want to open.
4. Open the folder and get messages from it. A folder may contain sub-folders, and you would want to recursively get messages from those folders as well.

In the phrase, we get a default instance of the `Session` object using the `getDefaultInstance()` static method. The `Session` object represents a mail session. With the `Session` object, we then get a `Store` object that implements the POP3 protocol. The `Store` object represents a message store and its access protocol. If, for example, we wanted to connect to an IMAP mail server instead of a POP3 server, we could change this line of code to get an IMAP store instead of the POP3 store. We'd also have to include an additional JAR file that supports the IMAP protocol. Sun provides the imap.jar file as part of the JavaMail distribution. We connect to a POP3 store by calling the `connect()` method of the `Store` object and passing a host, username, and password. In the remainder of the phrase, we retrieve the INBOX folder and all the messages contained within it. We print the message sender (From), the message subject, and the first 100 characters of the message body for each message in the INBOX folder.

The `Folder` class also contains a `list()` method, which we do not use in this phrase, but can be used to obtain an array of `Folder` objects representing all the subfolders of the folder on which it is called. So, for example, if the INBOX folder had many sub-folders, we could obtain a reference to each of those using the following code:

```
Folder folder = store.getFolder("INBOX");
folder.open(Folder.READ_ONLY);
Folder[] subfolders = folder.list();
```

The subfolders array in this example would contain a `Folder` object for each sub-folder under the INBOX folder. We could then process the messages in each of those, just as we did for the messages contained in the

INBOX folder. There is also a `getFolder()` method on the `Folder` class, which takes a single string parameter and returns a folder with a name matching the string passed in.

Using the `Folder` class, you could write a method that traversed an entire email account and read all messages contained in all of the user's folders.

13

Database Access

A database provides persistent storage for application data and is a critical part of many applications. Java has excellent support for accessing a relational database through the Java Database Connectivity (JDBC) API.

If your application has anything but a very simple data model with limited database access requirements, you might want to strongly consider using a database framework instead of writing directly to the JDBC API. The standard persistence framework for enterprise applications is the Enterprise Java Beans (EJB) framework. EJB is a part of the Java Enterprise Edition. EJB is considered to be overly complex by many Java developers, and thus open source alternatives are also becoming very popular. The complexity and problems with EJB fortunately have been partially addressed in EJB 3.0. EJB 3.0 is a big step in the right direction in terms of making EJB a more developer friendly technology. An excellent open source data persistence framework that is becoming very popular is the Hibernate framework. The Hibernate framework creates an object mapping layer of your relational data. The object mapping layer allows you to treat your persistent data in an object-oriented manner as opposed to through a procedural SQL interface. You can find more information about the Hibernate framework at: http://www.hibernate.org.

This chapter focuses purely on database access through JDBC. Even if you use a higher level persistence framework, it is important to have a good understanding of the JDBC API as this provides the foundation of most of the higher level frameworks.

Connecting to a Database via JDBC

```
Class.forName("sun.jdbc.odbc.JdbcOdbcDriver");
Connection conn =
   DriverManager.getConnection(url, user, password);
```

To make a database connection using JDBC, you first have to load a driver. In this phrase, we load the `JdbcOdbcDriver`. This driver provides connectivity to an ODBC data source. We load the driver using the `Class.forName()` method. Database JDBC drivers are generally provided by database vendors, although Sun does provide several generic drivers such as the ODBC driver that we use in this phrase. After we have the driver loaded, we get a connection to the database using the `DriverManager.getConnection()` method. We use a URL-like syntax to specify the database that you want to connect to. We also pass valid database login name and password. The URL must begin with the prefix `jdbc:`. After the prefix, the remainder of the URL specification format is vendor specific. The URL syntax for connecting to an ODBC database is shown here:

jdbc:odbc:databasename

Most drivers will require the URL string to include a hostname, a port, and a database name. For example, here is a valid URL for connecting to a MySQL database:

jdbc:mysql://db.myhost.com:3306/mydatabase

This URL specifies a MySQL database on the host `db.myhost.com`, connecting on port 3306, with the database name of `mydatabase`. The general format for a MySQL database URL is as follows:

jdbc:mysql://host:port/database

An alternative way of obtaining a database connection is through the use of JNDI. This is the approach you'd typically take if you were using an application server such as BEA WebLogic or IBM WebSphere.

```
Hashtable ht = new Hashtable();
ht.put(Context.INITIAL_CONTEXT_FACTORY,
     "weblogic.jndi.WLInitialContextFactory");
ht.put(Context.PROVIDER_URL, "t3://hostname:port");
Context ctx = new InitialContext(ht);
javax.sql.DataSource ds =
  (javax.sql.DataSource) ctx.lookup
("myDataSource");
Connection conn = ds.getConnection();
```

When using JNDI, we create an `InitialContext` instance and use that to look up a `DataSource`. We then get the connection from the data source object. There is also a version of the `getConnection()` method available that allows you to pass a user name and password to the database to get the connection for a database requiring user authentication.

It is important to always close a connection using the `Connection` class's `close()` method when you are finished using the `Connection` instance.

Sending a Query via JDBC

```
Statement stmt = conn.createStatement( );
ResultSet rs =
   stmt.executeQuery(
      "SELECT * from users where name='tim'");
```

In this phrase, we create a JDBC statement using the `Connection` object's `createStatement()` method and use it to execute a query that returns a Java `ResultSet`. To create a connection, see the previous phrase, "Connecting to a Database via JDBC." When performing a SELECT query, we use the `executeQuery()` method of the `Statement` object.

If we wanted to perform an UPDATE operation rather than a SELECT query, we would use the `executeUpdate()` method of the `Statement` object, instead of the `executeQuery()` method. The `executeUpdate()` method is used with SQL INSERT, UPDATE, and DELETE statements. The `executeUpdate()` method returns either the row count for INSERT, UPDATE or DELETE statements, or 0 for SQL statements that return nothing. Here is an example of how we would execute an UPDATE statement:

```
Statement stmt = conn.createStatement( );
int result =
   stmt.executeUpdate(
      "UPDATE users SET name='tim' where
      id='1234'");
```

It is important to remember that only one `ResultSet` object per `Statement` object can be open at the same time. All the execution methods in the `Statement` interface will close the current `ResultSet` object if there is an open one. This is important to remember if you are nesting database connections and queries. JDBC 3.0 introduced a feature called result set holdability. Holdability allows you to keep more than one result set open if you specify this option when the statement object is created. To learn more about the new features that were provided by JDBC 3.0, I'd recommend reading this article available on IBM's DeveloperWorks site: http://www-128.ibm.com/developerworks/java/library/j-jdbcnew/

When working with statements and results, it is important to always close the `Connection`, the `Statement`, and the `ResultSet` objects when finished with them. Each of the `Connection`, the `Statement`, and the `ResultSet` objects have a `close()` method used for performing a close operation to free up memory and release resources. Not closing these objects is a frequent cause of memory leaks in Java applications. Not closing a connection can also cause deadlock scenarios in multithreaded applications.

If you have a SQL statement that will be executed many times, it is more efficient to use a `PreparedStatement` query. See the next phrase "Using a Prepared Statement."

Using a Prepared Statement

```
PreparedStatement stmnt =
    conn.prepareStatement(
        "INSERT into users values (?,?,?,?)");
stmnt.setString(1, name);
stmnt.setString(2, password);
stmnt.setString(3, email);
stmnt.setInt(4, employeeId);
stmnt.executeUpdate( );
```

To create a prepared statement in JDBC, we use a `PreparedStatement` object in place of a `Statement` object. We pass the SQL into the `prepareStatement()` method on the `Connection` object. This creates a `PreparedStatement` object. When using a prepared statement, data values in the SQL statement are specified with a question mark. The actual values for these question mark placeholders are set later using the `PreparedStatement` set methods. The set methods available include `setArray()`, `setAsciiStream()`, `setBigDecimal()`, `setBinaryStream()`, `setBlob()`, `setBoolean()`, `setByte()`, `setBytes()`, `setCharacterStream()`, `setClob()`, `setDate()`, `setDouble()`, `setFloat()`, `setInt()`, `setLong()`, `setNull()`, `setObject()`, `setRef()`, `setShort()`, `setString()`, `setTime()`, `setTimestamp()`, and `setURL()`. Each of these set methods is used to set a different type of data as a parameter used in the SQL statement. For example, the `setInt()` method is used to set integer parameters, the `setString()` method is used to set String parameters, and so on.

In this phrase, we set three string values and one integer value, using the `setString()` and `setInt()` methods. For each question mark that appears in the query statement, there must be a corresponding set statement to set its value. The first parameter to the set statements specifies the position of the parameter being set from the query statement. For example, passing a value of `1` as the first parameter to a set statement will set the value of the first question mark position in the query statement. The second parameter to the set statements specifies the actual value being set. In our phrase, the variables `name`, `password`, and `email` are all assumed to be of type `String`. The `employeeId` variable is of type `int`.

When you are creating a SQL statement that you will reuse multiple times, it is more efficient to use a PreparedStatement instead of a regular Statement object. A prepared statement is a precompiled SQL statement, which makes it faster to execute repeatedly once it has been created.

Retrieving Results of a Query

```
ResultSet rs = stmt.executeQuery(
"SELECT name, password FROM users
 where name='tim'");
while (rs.next( )) {
    String name = rs.getString(1);
    String password = rs.getString(2);
}
```

A JDBC query returns a ResultSet object. A ResultSet represents a table of data containing the results of a database query. We can step through the ResultSet contents to get the results of the executed query. The ResultSet maintains a cursor that points to the current row of data. The ResultSet object has a next() method, which moves the cursor to the next row. The next() method will return false when there are no more rows in the ResultSet object. This makes it easy to use a while loop for stepping through all the rows contained within a ResultSet.

The ResultSet has getter methods for retrieving column values from the current row. Data values can be retrieved using either the index number of the column or the name of the column. Column numbering begins at 1. Column names as input to the getter methods are not case sensitive.

In this phrase, we obtain a `ResultSet` from executing a SELECT query. We loop through the rows contained within the `ResultSet` using the `next()` method and a while loop. We get name and password data values using the `getString()` method.

Remember, it is good practice to close your `ResultSet` instances when you are finished using them. A `ResultSet` object is automatically closed when the `Statement` object that generated it is closed, re-executed, or used to retrieve the next result from a sequence of multiple results.

Using a Stored Procedure

```
CallableStatment cs =
   conn.prepareCall("{ call ListAllUsers }");
ResultSet rs = cs.executeQuery( );
```

Stored procedures are database programs that are stored and maintained within the database itself. You can call one of these stored procedures from within Java using the `CallableStatement` interface and the `prepareCall()` method of the `Connection` object. A `CallableStatement` returns a `ResultSet` object just as a `Statement` or `PreparedStatement` does. In this phrase, we call the stored procedure `ListAllUsers` with no parameters.

A `CallableStatement` object can take input parameters also. Input parameters are handled exactly as they are when using a Prepared Statement. For example, here we show how you might call a stored procedure that uses input parameters:

```
CallableStatment cs =
   conn.prepareCall("{ call AddInts(?,?) }");
cs.setInt(1,10);
```

```
cs.setInt(2,50);
ResultSet rs = cs.executeQuery( );
```

Unlike other kinds of JDBC statements, a `CallableStatement` can also return parameters. These are referred to as OUT parameters. When using OUT parameters, the JDBC type of each OUT parameter must be registered before the `CallableStatement` object can be executed. The OUT parameters are registered using the `registerOutParameter()` method. After the statement has been executed, the OUT parameters can be retrieved using the `CallableStatement`'s getter methods.

```
CallableStatement cs =
   con.prepareCall("{call getData(?, ?)}");
cs.registerOutParameter(1, java.sql.Types.INT);
cs.registerOutParameter(2, java.sql.Types.STRING);
ResultSet rs = cs.executeQuery();
int intVal = cs.getInt(1);
String strVal = cs.getString(2);
```

In this example, we call a stored procedure named `getData()` which has two OUT parameters. One of these OUT parameters is an `int` value, and the other is a `String` value. After registering both of these parameters, we execute the query, and then get their values using the `getInt()` and `getString()` methods.

Another difference of functionality when using Stored Procedures is that a stored procedure can return multiple result sets. If a stored procedure returns more than one result set, the `getMoreResults()` method of the `CallableStatement` class is used to close the current result set and point to the next result set. The `getResultSet()` method is called after calling the `getMoreResults()` method to retrieve the result set being pointed to. An example that returns multiple result sets and uses these methods to retrieve each result set is shown below:

```
int i;
String s;
callablestmt.execute();
rs = callablestmt.getResultSet();
while (rs.next()) {
   i = rs.getInt(1);
}
callablestmt.getMoreResults();
rs = callablestmt.getResultSet();
while (rs.next()) {
   s = rs.getString(1);
}
rs.close();
callablestmt.close();
```

In this example, we set the `int` value `i` with results from the first result set and the `String` variable `s` with results from the second result set.

14

Using XML

XML, the Extensible Markup Language, is derived from the Standard Generalized Markup Language (SGML). Hypertext Markup Language (HTML) is also a markup language derived from SGML. XML is similar in most ways to HTML, with the exception that, in XML, you can define your own tags. You are not constrained to a predefined set of markup tags as you are in HTML. XHTML is a version of HTML that is XML compliant.

XML is commonly used as a general format for interchanging data across servers and applications. Common uses of XML include in business-to-business processes or storage of complex data such as a word processor document or even graphics files.

XML has gained wide acceptance across all industries and programming languages. Most programming languages now have some support for processing XML data. Java is no different in that respect. Java has excellent support available for processing XML documents—both creating and reading XML data.

This chapter assumes knowledge of XML. If you want to learn XML or brush up on your XML knowledge, a good book that is tailored to Java development is *Java and XML* by Brett McLaughlin and Justin Edelson. A new version of this book, the 3rd edition, should be available by the time you read this. The ISBN for this book is 059610149X.

Two common language-independent XML parsing APIs are defined by the World Wide Web Consortium (W3C). These are the DOM and SAX APIs. DOM, which stands for Document Object Model, is a parser that reads an entire XML document and builds a tree of Node objects, which is referred to as the DOM of a document. When using DOM, you end up with a complete parsed representation of the XML document and you can pull pieces of it out at any time. SAX, which stands for Simple API for XML, is not really a parser itself, but instead it is an API that defines an event handling mechanism that can be used to parse XML documents. When using SAX, you supply callback methods that are called by the SAX API when various elements of the XML document are encountered. A SAX implementation scans through an XML document calling the callback methods when it encounters the start and end of the various XML document elements. With SAX, the XML document is never fully stored or represented in memory.

Java's implementation of XML processing is referred to as the Java API for XML Processing, or JAXP. JAXP enables applications to parse and transform XML documents independent of a particular XML processing implementation. JAXP bundles both a DOM and a SAX parser and also includes an XSLT API for transforming XML documents. XSLT stands for Extensible Stylesheet Language Transformations. XSLT technology allows you to transform an XML document from one format into another. JAXP is a standard part of JDK 1.4 and later.

Parsing XML with SAX

```
XMLReader parser =
   XMLReaderFactory.createXMLReader(
         "org.apache.xerces.parsers.SAXParser");
parser.setContentHandler(new MyXMLHandler( ));
parser.parse("document.xml");
```

The SAX API works by scanning through an XML document from start to finish and providing callbacks for events that occur within the XML document. The events include things such as the start of an element, the end of an element, the start of an attribute, the end of an attribute, and so on. In this phrase, we create an `XMLReader` instance using the `SAXParser`. After we have created the parser instance, we then set a content handler using the `setContentHandler()` method. The content handler is a class that defines the various callback methods that will be called by the SAX parser when an XML document is parsed. In this phrase, we create an instance of `MyXMLHandler`, a class we then must implement, to serve as our handler. Finally, we call the `parse()` method, passing the name of an XML document and the SAX processing kicks off.

Here we show an example implementation of the `MyXMLHandler` class. The `DefaultHandler` class that we extend is a default base class for SAX event handlers.

```
class MyXMLHandler extends DefaultHandler {
   public void startElement(String uri,
                            String localName,
                            String qname,
                            Attributes attributes) {
```

```
      // process start of element
   }

   public void endElement(String uri,
                          String localName,
                          String qname) {
      // process end of element
   }

   public void characters(char[] ch,
                          int start,
                          int length) {
      // process characters
   }

   public MyXMLHandler( )
         throws org.xml.sax.SAXException {
      super( );
   }
}
```

In this example implementation, we implement only three methods—the `startElement()`, `endElement()`, and `characters()` methods. The `startElement()` method is called by the SAX parser when the start of an element in the XML document is encountered. Likewise, the `endElement()` method is called when the end of an element is encountered. The `characters()` method is called to notify of character data inside an element.

See the `DefaultHandler` JavaDoc for a complete description of all the methods that can be overridden in the SAX handler: http://java.sun.com/j2se/1.5.0/docs/api/org/xml/sax/helpers/DefaultHandler.html

In this phrase, the underlying Sax parser used is the Xerces parser. We set this parser in the method call shown below:

```
XMLReader parser =
   XMLReaderFactory.createXMLReader(
         "org.apache.xerces.parsers.SAXParser");
```

JAXP is designed to support pluggable parser implementations, and thus if you find a parser that you prefer over the Xerces parser, you can still use that with the code contained in this phrase. You do have to make sure that whatever parser implementation you are using is included in your class path.

SAX is generally more memory efficient than a DOM parser because with SAX, the entire XML document is not stored in memory all at once. The DOM API reads the entire document into memory and it is then processed in-memory.

Parsing XML with DOM

```
File file = new File("document.xml");
DocumentBuilderFactory f =
   DocumentBuilderFactory.newInstance();
DocumentBuilder p = f.newDocumentBuilder();
Document doc = p.parse(file);
```

The `DocumentBuilderFactory`, `DocumentBuilder`, and `Document` classes are the three classes that we use to kick off the parsing of an XML document using a DOM parser. We perform the parsing with the `DocumentBuilder` class. The `DocumentBuilder` class defines the API to obtain DOM `Document` instances from an XML document. The `DocumentBuilder` class can parse

XML from a variety of input sources, including `InputStreams`, `Files`, `URLs`, and `SAXInputSources`. In this phrase, we parse the XML from a `File` input source. The `parse()` method of the `DocumentBuilder` class parses the XML document and returns a `Document` object. A `Document` object represents the DOM of an XML document. From the `Document` instance, you could then pull the document apart and get at the components that make up the XML document, such as its entities, elements, attributes, etc.

The `Document` object is a container for a hierarchical collection of `Node` objects that represent the XML document's structure. Nodes can have a parent, children or attributes associated with them. There are three main subclasses of the `Node` type that represent the major parts of an XML document; these are the `Element`, `Text`, and `Attr` classes. Next, we show an example of further parsing a DOM using the `Document` class. Below is the sample XML document that we will use:

```
<Location>
  <Address>
    <City>Flat Rock</City>
    <State>Michigan</State>
  </Address>
</Location>
```

Assuming that we've already obtained a `Document` instance using the parse technique demonstrated in the previous phrase, the Java code here will pull out the city and state text values:

```
NodeList list =
   document.getElementsByTagName("City");
Element cityEl = (Element)list.item(0);
String city =
   ((Text)cityEl.getFirstChild()).getData();
```

```
NodeList list =
   document.getElementsByTagName("State");
Element stateEl = (Element)list.item(0);
String state =
   ((Text)stateEl.getFirstChild()).getData();
```

The method `getElementsByTagName()` that we use returns a `NodeList` containing all the elements matching the name passed in. Since our sample document contains only one City element and one State element, we just get the first (zero indexed) element out of the node list and cast it as an `Element` type. The City and State elements each have one child, which is a `Text` type. We use the `getData()` method of the `Text` type to get the actual value for the city and state.

Unlike a SAX parser, a DOM parser reads an entire XML document into memory, and the document is then parsed and processed from memory. In this regard, a SAX parser is more memory efficient because with SAX, the entire XML document is not stored in memory. The document is scanned in a streaming style when using SAX.

Using a DTD to Verify an XML Document

```
DocumentBuilderFactory factory =
   DocumentBuilderFactory.newInstance();
factory.setValidating(true);
DocumentBuilder builder =
   factory.newDocumentBuilder();
```

A Document Type Definition (DTD) file defines how a particular XML document type should be structured. For example, a DTD will specify which elements, attributes, and so on are permitted in a document. An XML document that conforms to a DTD is considered to be valid. An XML document that is syntactically correct, but does not conform to a DTD, is said to be well-formed.

To validate a document using a DTD, we simply need to call the `setValidating()` method of the `DocumentBuilderFactory` instance and pass a value of true. Any XML documents that we parse will then be validated against any DTDs that are specified in the XML document header. The following is a typical DTD declaration at the top of an XML document:

```
<!DOCTYPE people SYSTEM "file:baseball.dtd">
```

This declaration would attach the file `baseball.dtd` stored on the local file system as a DTD to the XML document in which it is declared.

When you specify DTD validation, if the XML document that you are parsing does not conform to the DTD, an exception will be thrown from the `parse()` method of the `DocumentBuilder` class.

A newer technology offering the same advantages of using a DTD is the XML Schema standard. An XML Schema defines an XML document's expected markup, just as a DTD does. One advantage of a schema document is that it is also an XML document, so you don't need yet another parser to read it, whereas a DTD is not a valid XML document itself. Instead of XML, DTDs are specified in XBNF (Extended Backus-Naur Form) grammar. To use a schema, you would use the `setSchema()` method of the `DocumentBuilderFactory` instead of the `setValidating()` method. This is shown here:

```
DocumentBuilderFactory factory =
   DocumentBuilderFactory.newInstance();
factory.setSchema(schema);
DocumentBuilder builder =
   factory.newDocumentBuilder();
```

The `setSchema()` method takes an instance of a `Schema` object. We will not go into detail on using schemas here, but see the `DocumentBuilderFactory`'s JavaDoc for more detail on implementing Schemas in Java: http://java.sun.com/j2se/1.5.0/docs/api/javax/xml/parsers/DocumentBuilderFactory.html

For more detailed information about schemas in general, see the Schema standard documentation at the following site: http://www.w3.org/TR/xmlschema-1/

Creating an XML Document with DOM

```
DocumentBuilderFactory fact =
   DocumentBuilderFactory.newInstance( );
DocumentBuilder builder =
   fact.newDocumentBuilder( );
Document doc = builder.newDocument( );
Element location = doc.createElement("Location");
doc.appendChild(location);
Element address = doc.createElement("Address");
location.appendChild(address);
Element city = doc.createElement("City");
address.appendChild(city);
line.appendChild(doc.createTextNode("Flat Rock"));
Element state = doc.createElement("State");
address.appendChild(state);
state.appendChild(doc.createTextNode("Michigan"));
((org.apache.crimson.tree.XmlDocument)doc).
     write(System.out);
```

In this phrase, we use the DOM API and JAXP to create an XML document. The XML segment created in this phrase is the following:

```
<Location>
  <Address>
    <City>Flat Rock</City>
    <State>Michigan</State>
  </Address>
</Location>
```

The main class we use here is the `org.w3c.dom.Document` class. This class represents the DOM of an XML document. We create an instance of the `Document` class using a `DocumentBuilder` obtained from a `DocumentBuilderFactory`. Each element of an XML document is represented in the DOM as an `Element` instance. In the XML document we are creating, we have build Location, Address, City, and State as `Element` object. We append the root level element, the Location, to the document object using the `Document` object's `appendChild()` method. The `Element` class also contains an `appendChild()` method that we use to build the hierarchy of the document beneath the root element.

It is also relatively simple to create an `Element` with attributes using the DOM API. For example, to add an attribute of `"id"` with a value of `"home"` to the Location element, we would use the following code:

```
location.setAttribute("id","home");
```

In this phrase, the underlying DOM parser used is the Crimson parser. In the phrase, this implementation shows up in the final line, also shown below.

```
((org.apache.crimson.tree.XmlDocument)doc).
      write(System.out);
```

JAXP is designed to support pluggable parser implementations, and thus if you find a parser that you prefer over the Crimson parser, you can still use that with the code contained in this phrase. You do have to make sure that whatever parser implementation you are using is included on your class path.

An alternative to using the JAXP API for working with XML is the JDOM API. JDOM is an open source project that is being standardized through the Java Community Process (JCP), under JSR 102. See http://www.jdom.org for more information about the JDOM API. JDOM provides a native Java API instead of the standard DOM API for reading and creating XML documents. Many find that JDOM is easier to use when creating XML documents than the DOM API.

Transforming XML with XSLT

```
StreamSource input =
   new StreamSource(new File("document.xml"));
StreamSource stylesheet =
   new StreamSource(new File("style.xsl"));
StreamResult output =
   new StreamResult(new File("out.xml"));
TransformerFactory tf =
   TransformerFactory.newInstance();
Transformer tx = tf.newTransformer(stylesheet);
tx.transform(input, output);
```

XSLT is a standard for transforming XML documents from one format to another using an XSL stylesheet. The `javax.xml.transform` package is the API for using the XSLT transformation standard in Java. XSL stands for Extensible Stylesheet Language. XSLT is XSL Transformation, and it allows you to completely restructure an XML document. In general, when using

XSLT, you have an input XML document and an input XSL stylesheet; together, these produce an output XML document. However, the output document type is not limited to XML. You can produce many types of output documents using an XSL transformation.

In this phrase, we create `StreamSource` instances for the documents, which are input into the transformation process. These are the XML document to be transformed and the XSL stylesheet that contains the transformation instructions. We also create a `StreamResult` object, which will be used to write the output document to. We then obtain an instance of a `Transformer` object, generated from a `TranformerFactory` instance. We pass the stylesheet stream into the `newTranformer()` method of the `TransformerFactory` object to create our `Transformer` object. Finally, we call the `transform()` method of the `Transformer` to transform our input XML document into the output document styled with the stylesheet we selected.

We don't go into details of what an XSL stylesheet looks like or how to create one. An excellent reference for learning more about XSL stylesheets and XSLT is *Java and XSLT* by Eric Burke.

XSL can be a powerful technology for developers. For example, suppose you have a web application that must be accessed from a variety of devices, including a PDA, a web browser on a PC, and a cell phone. Using XSLT, you could transform your output to a format suitable for each of these devices without having to specifically code output for each device type separately. XSLT is also very useful in creating multilingual sites. You can transform XML output into a variety of languages using XSLT transformations.

15

Using Threads

Threading is the way in which a software application carries on multiple processes at the same time. A thread in Java is a unit of program execution that runs concurrently with other threads.

Threads are commonly used in GUI applications. In a GUI application, one thread might be listening for input from the keyboard or other input devices, while another thread is processing the previous command. Networking is another common area in which you will find multithreading used. In network programming, one thread might be listening for connection requests, while another thread processes a previous request. Timers are also common uses of threads. A timer can be started as a thread running independently from the rest of an application. In all these examples, multithreading enables an application to carry on with processing while also executing another task that might take a longer amount of time and would cause long delays if not for multithreading.

Java has very good built-in support for writing multithreaded applications. Writing a multithreaded application was a very complex task in the C language, but in

Java, writing a multi-threaded application is a much easier task.

Starting a Thread

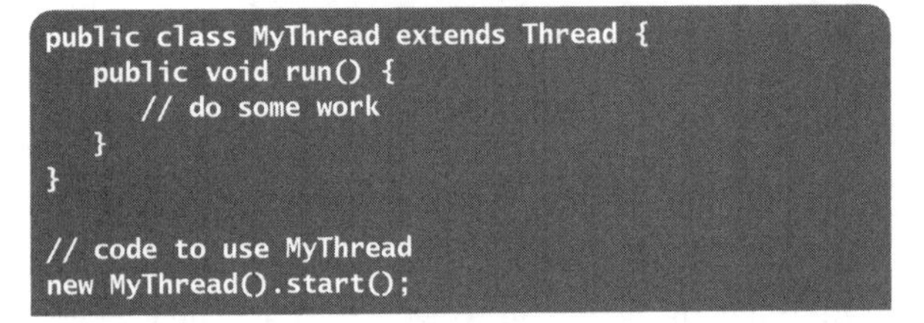

```
public class MyThread extends Thread {
   public void run() {
      // do some work
   }
}

// code to use MyThread
new MyThread().start();
```

There are two primary techniques for writing code that will run in a separate thread. You can either implement the `java.lang.Runnable` interface or extend the `java.lang.Thread` class. With either approach, you must implement a `run()` method. The `run()` method contains the code that you want to execute in the thread. In this phrase, we have extended the `java.lang.Thread` class. At the point where we want to start the thread, we instantiate our `MyThread` class and call the `start()` method, which is inherited from the `Thread` class.

Here, we show how running a thread is accomplished using the other technique of implementing the `Runnable` interface:

```
public class MyThread2 implements Runnable {
   public void run() {
      // do some work
   }
}

// code to use MyThread2
Thread t = new Thread(MyThread2);
t.start();
```

Implementing the Runnable interface is often used in situations in which you have a class that is already extending another class, so it cannot extend the Thread class. Java supports only single inheritance, making it impossible for a class to extend from two different classes. The method in which we start the thread is slightly different. Instead of instantiating the class we defined, as we did when we extended the Thread interface, here we instantiate a Thread object and pass our class that implements Runnable as a parameter to the Thread constructor. We then call the Thread's start() method, which starts the thread and schedules it for execution.

Anther common way of creating a thread is to implement the Runnable interface using an anonymous inner class. We show this method here:

```
public class MyThread3 {
   Thread t;

   public static void main(String argv[]) {
      new MyThread3();
   }

   public MyThread3() {
      t = new Thread(new Runnable( ) {
         public void run( ) {
            // do some work
         }
      });
      t.start( );
   }
}
```

In this example, all the code is contained within a single class, so it is well encapsulated; this makes it easy to see what is going on. Our Runnable implementation is defined as an inner class, rather than explicitly creating a class that implements the Runnable interface. This method is ideal for small run methods that don't require a lot of interaction with external classes.

Stopping a Thread

```
public class StoppableThread extends Thread {
   private boolean done = false;

   public void run( ) {
      while (!done) {
         System.out.println("Thread running");
         try {
            sleep(500);
         }
         catch (InterruptedException ex) {
            // do nothing
         }
      }
      System.out.println("Thread finished.");
   }

   public void shutDown( ) {
      done = true;
   }
}
```

If you want to create a thread that you can stop at some point prior to the completion of its execution—that is, the return from the run() method—the best way to do this is to use a boolean flag that you test at the top of a main loop. In this phrase, we create a thread by extending the Thread class with our StoppableThread class. Within the run() method, we have a while loop that checks the status of a boolean done flag. As long as the done flag remains false, the thread continues. To stop the thread, an external process could set the `done` flag to true, and this would cause the `while` loop in the `run()` method to exit and thus terminate this thread.

The `Thread` class does contain a `stop()` method, which some might be tempted to use to stop the thread, but Sun actually recommends against using this method. The reason is this: In case your thread is operating on any of your data structure objects and you suddenly call `stop()` on the thread, the objects will be left in an inconsistent state. In case any of your other threads are waiting for this particular object to be released, they will get stuck waiting forever. This might eventually lead to a deadlock situation. Also, the `stop()` method is deprecated in JDK 1.2 and later, so if you do use the `stop()` method in one of these JDKs, the compiler will generate deprecation warnings.

A good reference to the reasons why `stop()` is deprecated can be found here: http://java.sun.com/j2se/1.5.0/docs/guide/misc/threadPrimitiveDeprecation.html

Waiting For a Thread to Complete

```
Thread t = new Thread(MyThread);
t.start();
// do some other processing
t.join();
// continues after thread t completes
```

It might be the case that you want one thread of execution to wait for another thread to complete before continuing with the current thread. Joining threads is a common method of causing one thread to wait for the completion of another thread. For example, in this phrase, we start thread `t` from within the thread that is executing these lines of code. We then, in most cases, do some additional processing and call the `join()` method on the thread object when we want to stop execution of this thread and wait for the thread `t` to complete. Once thread `t` completes, execution will continue to the statements following the line in which we called the `join()` method. If the thread `t` were already completed when we called `join()`, the `join()` method would return immediately.

An alternative form of the `join()` method is available that takes a `long` parameter containing a value in milliseconds. When this method is used, the calling thread will wait up to a maximum of that number of milliseconds before continuing, even if the thread on which the `join()` method is called has not completed. To be complete, there is also a third implementation of the `join()` method that takes two parameters, a `long` value in milliseconds, and an `int` value in nanoseconds. This method behaves exactly as the single parameter version, except that the millisecond and nanosecond values are added together to determine the length of time the calling thread should wait before continuing. This gives you finer grained control over the wait time.

Synchronizing Threads

```
public synchronized void myMethod() {
   // do something
}
```

You perform synchronization when you want to protect sections of code from being accessed by more than one thread at a time. The `synchronized` keyword, which we show in this phrase, allows us to synchronize a method or code block so that only one thread at a time can execute this method or code block. In this phrase, if one thread is currently executing `myMethod()`, any other threads attempting to execute the same method, `myMethod()`, on the same object instance will be locked out of the method until the current thread completes execution and returns from `myMethod()`.

For non-static methods, the synchronization applies only to the object instance that another thread is executing the method on. Other threads may execute the same method, if it is called on a different instance. On the instance that is locked, the lock applies to all synchronized methods of that instance. No thread may call any synchronized methods on an instance for which one thread is already executing a synchronized method. For static methods, only one thread may execute the method at a time.

The `synchronized` keyword can also be applied to blocks of code. It does not have to cover a complete method. For example, the following block of code is synchronized using this technique:

```
synchronized(myObject) {
   // do something with myObject
}
```

When synchronizing a block of code, you also specify an object to synchronize on. It often makes sense to synchronize on the object containing the block of code, so you would pass the `this` object as the object being synchronized on, as shown here:

```
synchronized(this) {
   // do something
}
```

The object passed to the synchronized keyword is the object that is locked while a thread is executing the enclosed block of code.

Common places where you would want to use synchronization are where concurrent access by multiple threads might put shared data in an inconsistent state. You have probably heard the term thread-safe. A thread-safe class ensures that no thread uses an object that is in an inconsistent state. In the next block of code, we show an example of a class that could be problematic if we did not make this class thread-safe by using the `synchronized` keyword on the `adjust()` method. A class that has instance data members is often a sign of a class that can be problematic in a multithreaded environment. In this example, assume that two threads are running the `adjust()` method, and it is not synchronized. Thread A executes the line `size=size+1` and is interrupted after reading the `size` value, but before completing the reassignment to `size`. Thread B now executes and calls the `reset()` method. This method sets the `size` variable to `0`. Thread B is then interrupted returning control to thread A, thread A now continues executing the `size=size+1` statement, setting the value of `size` to be the value it was prior to being reset, with the addition of 1. The end result is that the `reset()` method will never appear to have been called. Its effects have been negated by the ill side effects of multithreading. By applying the `synchronized` keyword to these methods, we prevent this scenario by allowing only one thread to execute either of these methods at a time. The other thread will wait until the current thread has completed the method.

```
public class ThreadSafeClass {
   private int size;

   public synchronized void adjust() {
     size = size + 1;
      if (size >= 100) {
         size = 0;
      }
   }

   public synchronized void reset() {
      size = 0;
   }
}
```

Thread-safe programming only applies to an application that has multiple threads. If you are writing an application that does not use multithreading, you have nothing to worry about and do not need to concern yourself with the concept of thread-safe. Before making that decision though, keep in mind reuse of the application or component that you are writing as well. You might only use a single thread, but is it likely that another project will use your component in a multithreaded environment?

Synchronization can be used to make an object thread-safe, but bear in mind the performance tradeoff of using synchronized methods. Calling a synchronized method is substantially slower than calling a non-synchronized method because of the overhead of object locking. So, make sure you only synchronize methods that are truly required to be thread-safe.

Pausing a Thread

```
MyThread thread = new MyThread();
thread.start();
while (true) {

    // do work…

synchronized (thread) {
        thread.doWait = true;
    }

    // do work…

    synchronized (thread) {
        thread.doWait = false;
        thread.notify();
    }
}

class MyThread extends Thread {
    boolean doWait = false;
    public void run() {
        while (true) {
            // do work…
            synchronized (this) {
                while (doWait) {
                        wait();
                    }
                    catch (Exception e) {
                    }
                }
            }
        }
    }
}
```

This phrase shows you how to pause a thread from a different thread. In the phrase, we use the variable `doWait` as a flag to pause the execution of `MyThread`. In the `run()` method of `MyThread`, we check the `doWait` flag after performing some work in a loop to determine if we need to pause the thread's execution. If the doWait flag is set to true, we call the Object.wait() method to pause the thread's execution.

When we want to wake the thread up, we set the doWait flag to false and call the thread.Notify() method to wakeup the thread and continue its execution loop.

Having a thread pause itself is a simpler task. The code below shows how you would pause the current thread:

```
long numMilliSecondsToSleep = 5000;
Thread.sleep(numMilliSecondsToSleep);
```

This code would pause the current thread for 5000 milliseconds which is the equivalent of five seconds.

In addition to the methods described above, the Thread.suspend() and Thread.resume() methods provide a mechanism for pausing threads, however these methods have been deprecated. Use of these methods can often result in a deadlock. I only mention these methods so that you know to avoid using them. Because use of these methods is not recommended, they are not discussed any further here.

Listing All Threads

```
public static void listThreads() {
   ThreadGroup root = Thread.currentThread()
      .getThreadGroup().getParent();
   while (root.getParent() != null) {
      root = root.getParent();
   }
    visitGroup(root, 0);
}

public static void visitGroup(ThreadGroup group, int
level) {
```

```
   int numThreads = group.activeCount();
   Thread[] threads = new Thread[numThreads];
   group.enumerate(threads, false);
   for (int i=0; i<numThreads; i++) {
      Thread thread = threads[i];
      printThreadInfo(thread);
   }

   int numGroups = group.activeGroupCount();
   ThreadGroup[] groups = new
ThreadGroup[numGroups];
   numGroups = group.enumerate(groups, false);

   for (int i=0; i<numGroups; i++) {
      visitGroup(groups[i], level+1);
   }
}
private static void printThreadInfo(Thread t) {
   System.out.println("Thread: " + t.getName( ) +
               "  Priority: " + t.getPriority( ) +
               (t.isDaemon( )?" Daemon":"") +
               (t.isAlive( )?"":" Not Alive"));
}
```

In this phrase we list all running threads. All threads exist in a thread group, and each thread group can contain threads and other thread groups. The `ThreadGroup` class allows you to group threads and call methods on the `ThreadGroup` class that will affect all threads in the thread group. `ThreadGroups` can also contain child `ThreadGroups`. `ThreadGroups` organize all threads into a hierarchy.

In this phrase we iterate through all thread groups to print information about each thread. We start by finding the root thread group. We then use the `visitGroup()` method to recursively visit each thread group that exists under the root group. Within the `visitGroup()` method, we first enumerate all the threads contained in that group. We call the `printThreadInfo()` method, also contained in the phrase, to print the name, priority, daemon status, and alive status of each thread. After having iterated through all the threads in the current group, we enumerate all the groups contained within the current group and make a recursive call to the `visitGroup()` method for each group. This recursive method calling continues until all the groups and all the threads have been enumerated and information about each thread has been printed.

Thread groups are commonly used to group threads that are related or similar in some way, such as who created them, what function they perform, or when they should be started and stopped.

16

Dynamic Programming Through Reflection

Reflection is a mechanism for discovering data about a program at runtime. Reflection in Java enables you to discover information about fields, methods, and constructors of classes. You can also operate on the fields and methods that you discover. Reflection enables what is commonly referred to as dynamic programming in Java. Reflection in Java is accomplished using the Java Reflection API. This API consists of classes in the `java.lang` and the `java.lang.reflect` packages.

The things that you can do with the Java Reflection API include the following:

- Determine the class of an object
- Get information about a class's modifiers, fields, methods, constructors, and superclasses

- Find out what constants and method declarations belong to an interface
- Create an instance of a class whose name is not known until runtime
- Get and set the value of an object's field
- Invoke a method on an object
- Create a new array, whose size and component type are not known until runtime

The Java reflection API is commonly used to create development tools such as debuggers, class browsers, and GUI builders. Often in these types of tools, you need to interact with classes, objects, methods, and fields, and you do not know which ones at compile time. So the application must dynamically find and access these items.

Getting a Class Object

```
MyClass a = new MyClass();
a.getClass();
```

The most basic thing you usually do when doing reflective programming is to get a `Class` object. Once you have a `Class` object instance, you can obtain all sorts of information about the class and even manipulate the class. In this phrase, we use the `getClass()` method to get a `Class` object. This method of getting a `Class` object is often useful in situations in which you have the object instance but do not know what class it is an instance of.

There are several other ways of obtaining a `Class` object. If you have a class for which the type name is known at compile time, there is an even easier way of getting a class instance. You simply use the compiler keyword `.class`, as shown here:

```
Class aclass = String.class;
```

If the class name is not known at compile time, but is available at runtime, you can use the `forName()` method to obtain a `Class` object. For example, the following line of code will create a `Class` object associated with the `java.lang.Thread` class.

```
Class c = Class.forName("java.lang.Thread");
```

You can also use the `getSuperClass()` method on a `Class` object to obtain a `Class` object representing the superclass of the reflected class. For example, in the following code, `Class` object `a` reflects the `TextField` class, and `Class` object `b` reflects the `TextComponent` class because `TextComponent` is the superclass of `TextField`.

```
TextField textField = new TextField();
Class a = textField.getClass();
Class b = a.getSuperclass();
```

Getting a Class Name

```
Class c = someObject.getClass();
String s = c.getName();
```

Getting the name of a `Class` object is an easy task. You get the class name of any `Class` object using the `getName()` method. The `String` returned by the `getName()` method will be the fully qualified class name. So for example, if in this phrase, the `someObject` variable is an instance of the `String` class, the name returned from the call to `getName()` will be

```
java.lang.String
```

Discovering Class Modifiers

```
Class c = someObject.getClass();
int mods = c.getModifiers();
if (Modifier.isPublic(mods))
   System.out.println("public");
if (Modifier.isAbstract(mods))
   System.out.println("abstract");
if (Modifier.isFinal(mods))
   System.out.println("final");
```

In a class definition, keywords called modifiers can precede the `class` keyword. The modifiers available are: `public`, `abstract`, and `final`. To discover which modifiers have been applied to a given class, you first get a `Class` object representing that class using the `getClass()` method. Next, you would call the `getModifiers()` method on the class object to return a bitmapped `int` value representing the modifiers. You can then use static methods of the `java.lang.reflect.Modifier` class to determine which modifiers have been applied. The static methods available are: `isPublic()`, `isAbstract()`, and `isFinal()`.

NOTE: If you have a class object that may represent an `interface`, you might also want to use the `isInterface()` method. This method will return true if the modifiers passed in include the `interface` modifier.

The Modifier class also contains additional static methods for determining which modifiers have been applied to class methods and variables. These methods include: `isPrivate()`, `isProtected()`, `isStatic()`, `isSynchronized()`, `isVolatile()`, `isTransient()`, `isNative()`, and `isStrict()`.

Finding Superclasses

```
Class cls = obj.getClass();
Class superclass = cls.getSuperclass();
```

The ancestors of a given class are referred to as that class's superclasses. Using reflection, you can determine all of the ancestors of a given class. After you've obtained a `Class` object, you can use the `getSuperclass()` method to get the class's superclass if one exists. If a superclass exists, a `Class` object will be returned. If there is not a superclass, this method will return null. Remember that Java supports only single inheritance, so for any given class, there can be only one superclass. Actually to be clear, there can be only one direct superclass. Technically, all ancestor classes are considered to be superclasses of a given class. To retrieve all ancestor superclasses, you would recursively call the `getSuperclass()` method on each `Class` object that is returned.

The method shown here will print all the superclasses associated with the object passed in:

```
static void printSuperclasses(Object obj) {
   Class cls = obj.getClass();
   Class superclass = cls.getSuperclass();
   while (superclass != null) {
      String className = superclass.getName();
      System.out.println(className);
      cls = superclass;
```

```
        superclass = cls.getSuperclass();
    }
}
```

Often an Integrated Development Environment (IDE) such as Eclipse will include a class browser as a feature. The class browser allows the developer to visually navigate through a hierarchy of classes. This technique is one of the ways in which class browsers are constructed. In order to build a visual class browser, your application must be able to determine which classes are the superclasses of any given class.

Determining the Interfaces Implemented by a Class

```
Class c = someObject.getClass();
Class[] interfaces = c.getInterfaces();
for (int i = 0; i < interfaces.length; i++) {
    String interfaceName = interfaces[i].getName();
    System.out.println(interfaceName);
}
```

In the previous phrase, we show you how to find the superclasses associated with a given class. Superclasses are related to inheritance and the class extension mechanism in Java. In addition to extending a class, in Java you can implement an interface. Through reflection, you can also find which interfaces a given class has implemented. After you've obtained a `Class` object, you can use the `getInterfaces()` method to get the class's interfaces if indeed the class implements any interfaces. The `getInterfaces()` method will return an array of `Class` objects. Each object in the array represents one interface implemented by the given class. You can use the getName() method on these Class objects to get the name of the interfaces implemented.

Discovering Class Fields

```
Class c = someObject.getClass();
Field[] publicFields = c.getFields();
for (int i = 0; i < publicFields.length; i++) {
   String fieldName = publicFields[i].getName();
   Class fieldType = publicFields[i].getType();
   String fieldTypeStr = fieldType.getName();
   System.out.println("Name: " + fieldName);
   System.out.println("Type: " + fieldTypeStr);
}
```

You can discover the public fields that belong to a class by using the getFields() method on a Class object. The getFields() method returns an array of Field objects containing one object per accessible public field. The accessible public fields returned do not all have to be fields contained directly within the class you are working with. The following fields are also returned:

- Fields contained in a superclass
- Fields contained in an implemented interface
- Fields contained in an interface extended from an interface implemented by the class

Using the Field class, you can retrieve the field's name, type, and modifiers. In this phrase, we print out the name and type of each field. You can also get and set the value of a field. For more details on getting and setting the value of fields, see the phrases "Getting Field Values" and "Setting Field Values" also contained in this chapter.

You can also get an individual field instead of all the fields of an object if you know the field's name. The following example shows how you would get an individual field:

```
Class c = someObject.getClass();
Field titleField = c.getField("title");
```

In this example, we get a `Field` object representing the field with the name `"title"`.

The `getFields()` and `getField()` methods return only the public data members. If you want to get all the fields of a class including private and protected fields, you can use the `getDeclaredFields()` or `getDeclaredField()` methods. These methods behave like their `getFields()` and `getField()` counterparts except that they return all of the fields including private and protected fields.

Discovering Class Constructors

```
Class c = someObject.getClass();
Constructor[] constructors = c.getConstructors();
for (int i = 0; i < constructors.length; i++) {
   Class[] paramTypes =
      constructors[i].getParameterTypes();
   for (int k = 0; k < paramTypes.length; k ++) {
      String paramTypeStr = paramTypes[k].getName();
      System.out.print(paramTypeStr + " ");
   }
   System.out.println();
}
```

You can get information about a class's public constructors by calling the `getConstructors()` method on a `Class` object. This method returns an array of `Constructor` objects. Using the `Constructor` object, you can then get the constructor's name, modifiers, parameter types, and throwable exceptions. The `Constructor` object also has a `newInstance()` method that allows you to create a new instance of the constructor's class.

In this phrase, we get all the constructors for the `someObject` class. For each constructor found, we then get an array of `Class` objects representing all the parameters for that particular constructor. Finally, we print out each of the parameter types for each constructor.

NOTE: Note that the first constructor contained in the array of constructors returned will always be the default no argument constructor, if one exists. If no constructors exist, then the no argument constructor is defined by default.

You can also get an individual public constructor instead of all the constructors of an object if you know the constructor's parameter types. The following example shows how you would get an individual constructor:

```
Class c = someObject.getClass();
Class[] paramTypes = new Class[] {String.class};
Constructor aCnstrct = c.getConstructor(paramTypes);
```

In this example, we get a `Constructor` object representing the constructor that takes a single `String` parameter.

The `getConstructors()` and `getConstructor()` methods return only the public constructors. If you want to get all the constructors of a class including those that are private, you can use the `getDeclaredConstructors()` or getDeclaredConstructor() methods. These methods behave like their getConstructors() and getConstructor() counterparts except that they return all of the constructors including those that are private.

Discovering Method Information

```
Class c = someObject.getClass();
Method[] methods = c.getMethods();
for (int i = 0; i < methods.length; i++) {
   String methodName = methods[i].getName();
   System.out.println("Name: " + methodName);
   String returnType =
      methods[i].getReturnType().getName();
   System.out.println("Return Type: " + returnType);
   Class[] paramTypes =
      methods[i].getParameterTypes();
   System.out.print("Parameter Types:");
   for (int k = 0; k < paramTypes.length; k ++) {
      String paramTypeStr = paramTypes[k].getName();
      System.out.print(" " + paramTypeStr);
   }
   System.out.println();
}
```

You can get information about a class's public methods by calling the getMethods() method on a Class object. This method returns an array of Method objects. Using the Method object, you can then get the method's name, return type, parameter types, modifiers, and throwable exceptions. You can also use the Method.invoke() method to call the method. For more information about invoking methods, see the "Invoking Methods" phrase also in this chapter.

In this phrase, after getting the array of methods, we print the method name, the method's return type, and a list of the method's parameter types.

You can also get an individual public method instead of all the methods of an object if you know the method's name and parameter types. The following example shows how you would get an individual method:

```
Class c = someObject.getClass();
Class[] paramTypes =
   new Class[] {String.class, Integer.class};
Method meth = c.getMethod("setValues", paramTypes);
```

In this example, we get a `Method` object representing the method with the name `setValue` and taking two parameters, a `String` and an `Integer`.

The methods we've discussed so far, `getMethods()` and `getMethod()`, return all the public methods that can be access through the class. Corresponding methods are available to get all methods regardless of their access type. The methods `getDeclaredMethods()` and `getDeclaredMethod()` behave exactly like their counterparts, except that they return all the class's methods, regardless of access type. This allows you to get even private methods.

Often an Integrated Development Environment (IDE) such as Eclipse will include a class browser as a feature. The class browser allows the developer to visually navigate through a hierarchy of classes. This technique is one of the ways in which class browsers are constructed. In order to build a visual class browser, your application must have a way of knowing all the methods of any given class.

Getting Field Values

```
Class c = anObject.getClass();
Field titleField = c.getField("title");
String titleVal = (String) titleField.get(anObject);
```

In order to get a field value, you must first get a `Field` object for the field you want to obtain the value of. See the phrase "Discovering Class Fields" earlier in this chapter for more information about getting `Field` objects from a class.

The `Field` class has specialized methods for getting the values of primitive types. Methods such as `getInt()`, `getFloat()`, and `getByte()` allow you to get the values of the primitive types. For complete details of the getter methods available on the `Field` object, see the JavaDoc at: http://java.sun.com/j2se/1.5.0/docs/api/java/lang/reflect/Field.html.

To get fields that are stored as objects rather than primitives, you use the more general `get()` method and cast the return result to the correct object type. In this phrase, we get the field named `"title"`. After getting the field as a `Field` object, we then get the field's value using the `get()` method and casting the result as a `String` type.

In this phrase, we knew the name of the field that we wanted to get the value for. We could get the value of a field even if we didn't know its name at compile time by combining this phrase with the "Discovering Class Fields" phrase. In that phrase, we show how to get field names. This technique could be useful in a tool such as a GUI builder, where you want to get the value of various GUI object fields, and the field names are not known until runtime.

Setting Field Values

```
String newTitle = "President";
Class c = someObject.getClass();
Field titleField = c.getField("title");
titleField.set(someObject, newTitle);
```

In order to set a field value, you must first get a `Field` object for the field you want to set the value of. See the phrase "Discovering Class Fields" in this chapter for more information about getting `Field` objects from a class. You should also refer to the phrase "Getting Field Values" also contained in this chapter for more information about getting field values.

The `Field` class has specialized methods for setting the values of primitive types. Methods such as `setInt()`, `setFloat()`, and `setByte()` allow you to set the values of the primitive types. For complete details of the set methods available on the `Field` object, see the JavaDoc at: http://java.sun.com/j2se/1.5.0/docs/api/java/lang/reflect/Field.html.

To set fields that are stored as objects rather than primitives, you use the more general `set()` method, passing the object instance for which you are setting field values and the value of the field as an object. In this phrase, we set the field named `"title"`. After getting the field as a `Field` object, we then set the field's value using `set()`, passing the object instance we are setting field values on and the new value for the title string.

In this phrase, we knew the name of the field that we wanted to set the value for. We could set the value of a field even if we didn't know its name at compile time by combining this phrase with the "Discovering Class Fields" phrase presented earlier in this chapter. In that phrase, we show how to get field names. This technique could be useful in a tool such as a GUI builder, where you want to set the value of various GUI object fields, and the field names are not known until runtime.

Often, a debugger will let you change the value of a field during a debugging session. To implement a feature like that, the developer of the debugger would use this technique to set the fields value since the developer would not know which field's value you were setting at compile time.

Invoking Methods

```
Baseball bbObj = new Baseball();
Class c = Baseball.class;
Class[] paramTypes =
   new Class[] {int.class, int.class};
Method calcMeth =
   c.getMethod("calcBatAvg", paramTypes);
Object[] args =
   new Object[] {new Integer(30), new Integer(100)};
Float result = (Float) calcMeth.invoke(bbObj, args);
```

The reflection API allows you to dynamically invoke methods even if the method name that you want to invoke is not known at compile time. In order to invoke a method, you must first get a `Method` object for the method that you want to invoke. See the phrase "Discovering Method Information" earlier in this chapter for more information about getting `Method` objects from a class.

In this phrase, we are trying to invoke a method that calculates a baseball batting average. The method is called `calcBatAvg()`, and it takes two integer parameters, a batter's hit count, and at-bat count. The method returns a batting average as a `Float` object. We invoke the method `calcBatAvg()` using the following steps:

- Get a `Method` object associated with the calcBatAvg() method from the `Class` object that represents the `Baseball` class.

- Invoke the calcBatAvg() method using the `invoke()` method on the `Method` object. The `invoke()` method takes two parameters: The first is an object whose class declares or inherits the method, and the second is an array of parameter values to be passed to the invoked method. If the method is a static method, the first parameter will be ignored and might be null. If the method does not take any parameters, the argument array might be of zero length, or null.

In the case of our phrase, we pass an instance of the `Baseball` object as the first parameter to the `invoke()` method and an object array containing two wrapped integer values as our second parameter. The return value returned from the `invoke ()` method will be the value returned from the method being invoked, in this case the calcBatAvg() return value. If the method returns a primitive, the value will first be wrapped in as an object and returned as an object. If the method has a return type of void, a null will be returned. The `calcBatAvg()` method returns a `Float` value, so we cast the returned object to be a `Float` object.

An example of where this technique would be useful is in the implementation of a debugger that allows a user to select a method and invoke it. Since the method being selected is not known until runtime, this reflective technique would be used to invoke that method.

Loading and Instantiating a Class Dynamically

```
Class personClass = Class.forName(personClassName);
Object personObject = personClass.newInstance();
Person person = (Person)personObject;
```

Using the `Class.forName()` and the `newInstance()` methods of a `Class` object, you can dynamically load and instantiate a class when you don't know the class's name until runtime. In this phrase, we load the class using the `Class.forName()` method, passing the name of the class we want to load. This returns a `Class` object. We then call the `newInstance()` method on the `Class` object to instantiate an instance of the class. The `newInstance()` method returns a generic `Object` type, so in the last line, we cast the returned object to be the type we are expecting to have.

This phrase is particularly useful in the scenario in which you have one class that extends a base class or implements an interface, and you might want to store the name of the extension or implementation class in a configuration file. This would allow the end user to dynamically plug in different implementations without having to recompile the application. For example, if we had the code from the phrase in our application, and the following code in a plug-in to the application, we could have the application dynamically instantiate a `BusinessPerson` object at runtime by specifying the full class name of the `BusinessPerson` object in a configuration file. Before executing our phrase, we would read the class name from the configuration file and set the `personClassName` variable to that value.

```
public class BusinessPerson extends Person {
 //class body, extends the behaviour of Person class
}
```

The application code in this case would have no hard-coded references to the actual `BusinessPerson` class. As a result, in your application you only have to hard-code the more generic base class or interface, and you can dynamically configure a specific implementation at run-time by editing a configuration file.

17

Packaging and Documenting Classes

A Java application will typically consist of many classes, sometimes hundreds, or even thousands of classes. Because Java requires each public class to be defined in a separate file, you end up with at least as many files as you have classes. This can easily become unmanageable when it comes to working with your classes, finding files, or installing and distributing your application. Fortunately, this was considered when Java was created, and Sun has defined a standard packaging mechanism for placing related classes into packages. Packages in Java are a way of organizing classes according to functionality. The packaging mechanism also organizes Java source files into a known directory structure based on the package names used.

There is also a standard mechanism in Java for packaging Java classes into standard archive files. Applications can be executed directly from the archive file, or libraries can be distributed as an archive. The standard

Java archive file is the JAR file, and these files end with a `.jar` extension. The JAR file uses the Zip archive protocol, and JAR files can be extracted using any tool that supports unzipping an archive. Sun also provides the jar tool for creating and expanding JAR archives. The jar tool is part of the standard JDK distribution. JAR stands for Java Archive.

Creating a Package

```
package com.timothyfisher.book;
```

In a large application or library, Java classes are usually organized into packages. To put a class into a package, you simply include a package statement, such as the one shown in this phrase, at the beginning of the class file. The package statement must be the first non-comment line of a class file. The example in this phrase would assign the class contained in the file to the package `com.timothyfisher.book`.

The package name of a class becomes a part of its full name. For example, if we had a class named `MathBook` in the `com.timothyfisher.book` package, the fully specified class name would be `com.timothyfisher.book.MathBook`. Package names also dictate the directory structure in which the class source files are stored. Each element of the path name represents a directory. For example, if your source code root directory is at `project/src`, the source code for the `MathBook` class would be stored in the following directory path:

```
project/src/com/timothyfisher/book/
```

The Java standard libraries are all organized into packages that you are most likely familiar with. These packages include `java.io`, `java.lang`, `java.util`, and so on.

Classes stored in a package can also be easily imported into a file. For example, you can import an entire package into your Java source file with the following syntax:

```
import java.util.*;
```

This import statement will import all the classes contained in the `java.util` package. Be aware, though, that this will not import classes contained in packages beneath `java.util`, such as those contained in the package `java.util.logging`. A separate import statement is needed to also import those classes.

Java 5.0 introduced a new feature related to importing classes called static imports. A static import allows you to import static members from classes, allowing them to be used without class qualification. For example, to reference the `cos()` method in the `java.lang.Math` package, you would have to refer to it as follows:

```
double val = Math.cos(90);
```

If you import the `java.lang.Math` package using a static import like this:

```
import static java.lang.Math.*;
```

you can refer to the `cos()` method as follows:

```
double val = cos(90);
```

When executing a Java application from the command line using the Java executable, you must include the full package name when specifying the main executable class. For example, to run a `main()` method in the `MathBook` example discussed previously, you would type the following:

```
java com.timothyfisher.book.MathBook
```

This command would be executed from the root of the package structure. In this case, the directory above the `com` directory.

Classes that are not specifically assigned to a package using a package statement are considered to be included in a "default" package. It is a good practice to always put your classes in packages that you define. Classes that are in the default package can not be imported or used within classes in other packages.

Documenting Classes with JavaDoc

```
javadoc -d \home\html
        -sourcepath \home\src
        -subpackages java.net
```

JavaDoc is a tool for generating API documentation in HTML format from comments placed in Java source code files. The JavaDoc tool is a standard part of the JDK installation. In this phrase, we show one sample usage of the JavaDoc tool. JavaDoc has many command-line options and flags that can be used to document classes and packages. For a full description of the options available when using JavaDoc, refer to the Sun documentation at: http://java.sun.com/j2se/1.5.0/docs/guide/javadoc/index.html.

The javadoc command used in this phrase will generate JavaDoc documentation for all classes contained in the java.net package and all of its subpackages. The source code is assumed to be in the \home\src directory. The output of the command will be written to the \home\html directory.

Inside a Java source file, a typical JavaDoc comment looks like this:

```
/**
 * A comment describing a class or method
 *
 * Special tags preceded with the @ character to
 * document method parameters, return types,
 * Method or class author name, etc.  Below is an
 * example of a parameter being documented.
 * @parameter input The input data for this method.
 */
```

The /** and */ character sequences denote the beginning and end of a JavaDoc comment.

The output of the JavaDoc tool is the standard Java class documentation that you are most likely used to seeing if you've viewed any Java documentation online in the past. The JDK itself is thoroughly documented using JavaDoc documentation. You can view the JavaDoc for the JDK at: http://java.sun.com/j2se/1.5.0/docs/api/index.html

JavaDoc generated documentation makes it easy to browse through the classes that make up an application or library. An index page is provided that indexes all the classes with hyperlinks to each class. Indexes are also provided for each package.

It is common to integrate the creation of JavaDoc documentation with an application's build process. So, for example, if you are using the Ant build tool, there is an Ant task available for generating JavaDoc as part of your build.

The technology that enables JavaDoc to work has also been used recently to create other tools to perform tasks that go beyond just documenting Java files. The Doclet API powers JavaDoc and these third-party tools. One of the most popular third-party uses of the Doclet API is the open source project XDoclet. XDoclet is an engine that enables attribute-oriented programming. With XDoclet, you can add metadata to your source code to automate tasks such as EJB creation. To find out more about XDoclet, you can find it online at: http://xdoclet.sourceforge.net/.

Another API for working with JavaDoc style comments that is part of standard Java is the Taglet API. Using the Taglet API, you create programs called Taglets. Taglets can modify and format JavaDoc style comments contained in your source files. For more information about the Taglet API see: http://java.sun.com/j2se/1.4.2/docs/tooldocs/javadoc/taglet/overview.html

Archiving Classes with Jar

```
jar cf project.jar *.class
```

The jar utility is included with the JDK, and is used to package groups of classes into a bundle. Using the jar tool, you can create, update, extract, list, and index a JAR file. In this phrase, all the classes contained in the current directory from which the jar command is run will be put into a JAR file with the name `project.jar`. The `c` option tells the jar utility to create a new archive file. The `f` option is always followed by a filename specifying the name of the JAR file to use.

Complete applications can be distributed as JAR files. Applications can also be executed out of a JAR file without having to first extract them. See the phrase "Running a Program from a JAR File" contained in this chapter for more information about doing this.

All classes contained in a JAR file can be easily included on the CLASSPATH when running or compiling a Java application or library. To include the contents of a JAR file in the CLASSPATH, you simply include the path to the JAR file instead of a directory. For example, your CLASSPATH statement might be similar to the following:

```
CLASSPATH=.;c:\projects\fisher.jar;c:\projects\
classes
```

This would include all the classes contained in the archive `fisher.jar` in your CLASSPATH. It is important to note that to include the classes in a JAR file, you must specify the name of the JAR file in the classpath. You cannot just point to a directory containing multiple JAR files as you can for .class files.

For more detailed information about using the jar tool, refer to the official JAR documentation from Sun available at: http://java.sun.com/j2se/1.5.0/docs/guide/jar/index.html.

Running a Program from a JAR File

```
java -jar Scorebook.jar
```

Using the java command-line executable, you can execute a Java application that is packaged in a JAR file. To do this, you use the `-jar` switch when running the `java` command. You must also specify the name of the JAR file that contains the application you want to execute.

You must specify the class containing the `main()` method that you want to execute in a manifest file. For example, to execute the `com.timothyfisher.Scorebook` class, you would use a manifest file with the following contents:

```
Manifest-Version: 1.2
Main-Class: com.timothyfisher.Scorebook
Created-By: 1.4 (Sun Microsystems Inc.)
```

The manifest file is placed in the JAR file along with your classes.

This functionality allows Java developers to be able to distribute an application in a single JAR file and include a script file such as a Windows BAT file, or a UNIX shell script that can be used to launch the application using syntax similar to what is shown in this phrase.

Index

D

G

H

I

J-K

S

T

U-V

W

X

Y-Z

THIS BOOK IS SAFARI ENABLED

INCLUDES FREE 45-DAY ACCESS TO THE ONLINE EDITION

The Safari® Enabled icon on the cover of your favorite technology book means the book is available through Safari Bookshelf. When you buy this book, you get free access to the online edition for 45 days.

Safari Bookshelf is an electronic reference library that lets you easily search thousands of technical books, find code samples, download chapters, and access technical information whenever and wherever you need it.

TO GAIN 45-DAY SAFARI ENABLED ACCESS TO THIS BOOK:

- Go to **http://www.samspublishing.com/safarienabled**
- Complete the brief registration form
- Enter the coupon code found in the front of this book on the "Copyright" page

If you have difficulty registering on Safari Bookshelf or accessing the online edition, please e-mail customer-service@safaribooksonline.com.